Emotional Inte

C000255429

*The Essential Beginn̲ ̲ ̲ ̲ ̲ to
Mastering Social Skills, Improve
Relationships and Control
Emotions
(Social Skills, Anger Management,
Enneagram, and Self-Discipline)*

Table of Contents

Introduction

Hello and thank you for downloading *Emotional Intelligence*: *The Essential Beginners Guide to Mastering Social Skills, Improve Relationships and Control Emotions (Social Skills, Anger Management, Enneagram, and Self-Discipline)* and thank you for doing so.

The purpose of this book is to introduce you to Emotional Intelligence as a guide for beginners who may have never heard or known about what emotional intelligence is, or those readers who are aware of it is and are interested in learning more about it.

Emotional intelligence has been incorporated into the workplace since the 1990s. Since then, professional emotional intelligence is probably as vital as IQ (technical skill) for success in the workplace. Many corporations today are understanding that hiring people who have a degree and the technical ability to do a job is not enough to fill a position properly. They now realize the effect of people who have high emotional intelligence levels are more productive which benefits an organization and the productivity of the organization.

The following chapters will discuss what Emotional Intelligence is, how developing self-awareness of our emotions, self-management, the control of our emotions, social awareness, the ability to recognize the emotions of other people and relationship awareness, the ability to have healthy and successful personal and professional relationships.

There are plenty of books on this subject on the market, thanks again for choosing this one! Every effort was made to ensure it is full of as much useful information as possible. Please enjoy!

Chapter 1: What Is Emotional Intelligence – How to Know If We Have It and How to Acquire It

Emotional Intelligence – What Is It?

Emotional intelligence is one of many different kinds of intelligence. There is the intelligence quotient that we know as IQ which is the ability to recover, remember items from memory and logical reasoning. There is also a new intelligence curiosity quotient known as CQ and refers to the ability to have the incentive to learn a specific subject.

Emotional intelligence, also known as EQ, is a person having the aptitude to recognize, understand and manage emotions and recognize, understand and sway the emotions of others. Emotions can motivate our own behavior as well as influence people, positively as well as negatively. It is about how to become knowledgeable in coping with our emotions and the emotions of others, particularly when our emotions are under pressure.

People are emotional. There are different types of emotion and the levels of expressing them from very mild to extremely intense, and for some, totally out of control. We make emotional decisions and respond to inducements based on emotion. Our capability to develop in EQ has a tremendous impact on how we make decisions, recognize opportunities and our relationships. Having EQ is a very important characteristic to have. (Connors, 2018)

This is a guide to those who are beginners in comprehending and developing emotional intelligence. You may already have emotional awareness and intelligence yet have never "identified" what you innately have within you. As each characteristic is explained, you may then be able to correlate each of these aspects of emotional intelligence with yourself.

There are a number of qualities that make up emotional intelligence. Some people have an abundance of these qualities, while others lack many, if not all and are devoid of emotion or the ability to recognize how their decisions or reactions and interactions with others can be inappropriate because of their inability to acknowledge emotions.

These are qualities that emotionally intelligent people possess:

Ability to have Self-Awareness - The ability to recognize what inducements you are being faced with, understanding yourself and planning how to manage yourself both proactively and reactively. How we view ourselves and how we recognize others to see us. This second aspect of self-awareness is probably the hardest to correctly evaluate.
Inquire within yourself and ask self-examining questions as well as others for feedback in a caring, truthful setting. (Connors, 2018)

Be Curious - Passionate people are curious people. They ask questions of themselves, of how things work, and of others. When you are curious, you desire to be your best. Your "feelers" are up, craving to grow and acquire more knowledge. The mindset of learning more is a positive effect and touches others and other areas of your life.

Persons that have a high CQ are usually more accepting of inexactness. This urbane style of thinking is the definition of complexity. CQ lends itself to elevated levels of intelligent investment and acquiring knowledge.

Have Empathy – Empathy is the capability to comprehend or feel what another person is enduring from within their perspective and perception. It is the ability to put yourself in another person's position.

There are two different kinds of empathy. One is *affective empathy,* the feelings we get in our reaction to another person's emotions. Mirroring the person's feelings, or sensing the other's anxiety, stress or fear is what defines affective empathy. *Cognitive empathy*, also known as *perspective taking* is the ability to recognize and identify with another person's feelings.

We are able to empathize based on our reaction to others. If you have stowed away in your memory your own feelings that make you feel reactive as well as in perspective, you can learn to be empathetic. Consider and examine these emotions and decide how you would want to treat other people as you would want to be treated. (Connors, 2018)

Have an Analytical Mind – People who analyze and process new information that is presented while continuing to analyze old information and ways of doing things, looking to see if there are ways for improvement are emotionally intelligent.

Those who have a high EQ are able to solve problems and think about the way we do what we do, and the way of being. A healthy desire for an incessantly improving mindset focused on being open to new ideas as well as bettering yourself is what it is to have an analytical mind. (Connors, 2018)

Wants and Needs

Someone who is emotionally intelligent is able to differentiate between things that are needed versus things that are nice to have, or another word for this is luxuries or treats, not necessary to one's life. Needs are the things needed to survive, provide for our safety and our nourishment. When these needs are met, then move on to other needs and wants.

We may want a Porsche or other type of luxury car, a second vacation home or a state-of-the-art iPhone. These are not necessarily needs and aren't needed to exist and survive, but they are wanted because we desire them or what we think matters to society. Drawing a clear difference between what you need and what you want will help you to distinguish what is needed to live and what you may desire but is not needed.

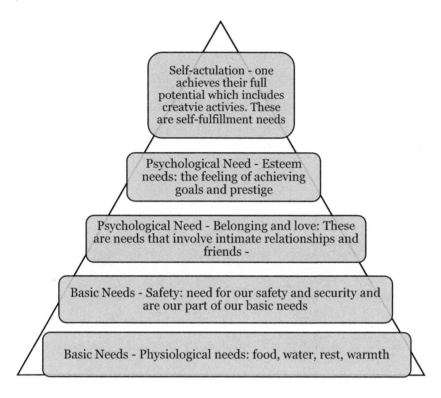

Hierarchy of Needs – Abraham Maslow

Emotionally intelligent people can distinguish the difference between the two mindsets and determine before they fulfill their wants. (Connors, 2018)

Our Belief – a key component in the ability to manage emotional self-control is the power of faith to believe in yourself in the immediate and well as futuristically. It is the belief that the situations that are and the people who are in your life are there for a reason and that, in the end, all eventually turns out for good.

Our belief and faith is not the only thing that helps you. It also takes action. When the combination of values such as perseverance, a positive attitude, and hard work and faith, a strong, winning foundation is established. Great thinkers and leaders use faith either spiritually, emotionally or applied context.

Meditating helps you to think about ways you can develop a belief in yourself. Effect a greater faith for the person you are and who you want to grow to be. Pieces of your life will come together. Believe and trust that you will be able to live your life joyfully. (Connors, 2018)

Be Passionate – having a passion and purpose are what people with a high EQ use to light up the engine that motivates them to do what they do. The passion is contagious and infective and infiltrates all areas of their lives as well as inspires people around them.

Passion is an indefinable quality that gives something a distinctive feel to it. When you feel it or can see others exude it, you know that it's passional. It gives one an instinct, ambition, desire that is naturally felt and motivates a love for someone or something. Passion helps inspire and sustain us and brings positive energy to keep going. Emotionally intelligent people are willing to carry on and go forward regardless of any circumstances. This is what makes emotionally intelligent people passionate. (Connors, 2018)

Be Adaptable – People who recognize when to continue the route or course they are on, and when it's time to change that course have emotional intelligence. When there is an ability to recognize the importance in making quick, snap decisions that are in your best interest, is called adaptability. You need to decide whether you continue in the direction you've been going or change your direction as you move forward.

Likewise, when one plan is not working, try reevaluating and deciding whether another angle will work. Always stay open-minded and willing to be adaptable.
New elements can be introduced to an established routine. Be adaptable in the way you treat others and yourself, as well as what you do and how you think.

Life will always throw the curveballs that will necessitate you to make assessments and changes in the course of your life and if you will be successful and happy if you choose one course to take or another. Realize that you have the ability to change your course if you wish. Or, you can start over, although it may not be the best or wisest decision. You are the only one who truly knows what is or what isn't. Begin by leaving that option open. (Connors, 2018)

Be Optimistic – be positive if you want to boost your opportunities, think constructively and clearly and develop your relationships, have an optimistic, positive attitude. Our attitude is the main thing that is always in our control. It is what we try to manage and influence. Having a positive, optimistic attitude is a choice we can make every day.

When we have a positive mindset, we are motivated and smarter. This is the attitude that is attributed to success. A positive, optimistic attitude attracts people who want to be near and around this sensation. We feel we have the ability to succeed in what we do and how we do it.

Help Others to Succeed and You Will Succeed - Emotionally intelligent people have an interest in achievement and success. However, it's not just their success they want to achieve – they want to help others achieve their success as well. Their spirit, leadership, and optimism motivate them to do the best for themselves and others are what displays their emotional intelligence. It's not all about them; it's about everyone.

Often, we have narrow vision and are self-absorbed with what's going on in "our world" and not conscious about others around us. This is a concern and it must be addressed. Yes, we want to succeed, and we should be focused on ourselves, but at the same time, we should be aware of people around us who want to succeed as well. We should maintain a desire to want to see that these people succeed, just as we want to succeed as well.

This spirit of helping others is a good way of warding off the possible envy and greed that sometimes arises when one person is successful while others struggle to achieve the same success. It also helps us to invigorate our passion and motivates us toward the achievement of the next goal we are aiming for. It helps us to benefit from gaining allies and build strong relationships that will be reciprocated. (Connors, 2018)

Many of us probably think that we know our own feelings, as well as those of others and tend to overestimate how emotionally intelligent we are. We may know our own feelings, but don't take the time to focus on the feelings of others. This doesn't mean that we do this to specifically ignore our fellow human beings, but it's easy to be short-sighted in what emotions others may be feeling without really meaning to.

It's important to be able to know our own feelings AND to understand and respond to the feelings of others. It is an important factor in our happiness, health, professional and personal success.

The following chapters will outline the types of emotions that we experience, the most powerful being anger, how to control our feelings, self-discipline, how to have great relationships, an all-important communication in the workplace, how to boost your emotional intelligence and the benefits that come with being emotionally intelligent. There's also an EQ test that will give you an idea of how emotionally intelligent you are.

Emotional intelligence is about being informed and knowledgeable you're your feelings and attuned to the feelings of others. It's about using your emotions to enlighten your thinking. Emotional intelligence can be learned and open vistas for you that you may not have been aware of or did not know how to develop. Use this book as a guide to help you develop your emotional intelligence and being more in touch with yourself and others.

Chapter 2: Anger Management – How to Control and Manage Your Anger with Anger Management Techniques

Anger, a basic human emotion that is experienced by everyone. It is triggered by an unpleasant situation, hurt, annoyance, mistreatment, a betrayal or stress. Anger is a strong emotion and sometimes hard to control. Some people can express their anger, take a short break to retreat and regroup, recover and move on. Others harbor their anger long after the person or event that triggered their anger is long over and hold on to their anger, sometimes for years.

As children, we are exposed to how the adults around us express their anger. We copy this behavior. Today, there is an anxious and uneasy association with anger expression. Many people, through their upbringing, think it is improper to directly express anger. They are taught that anger is intolerable and dangerous. These people have a distrust of anger, repress or ignore it and then express their anger indirectly or use it as a weapon against others.

The anger threshold varies for each of us. Anger for some people it is slow in coming, but explosive when it finally is exhibited. Instantaneous anger is how other people display their anger. It happens immediately and without warning, triggered by what would be considered as small and incidental by some but enormously off-putting to those whose anger flares at the bat of an eye. Some people seldom feel angry while others always get angry.

There are experts who suggest that the rate of which an average adult feels anger is about once a day while feeling annoyed is about three times per day. There is also a viewpoint expressed by anger management specialists that suggest getting angry fifteen times a day is a realistic average. (Mills, 2019)

Anger is an emotion that can, when controlled and managed, can be constructive, while unmanaged, off-the-rail anger can be extremely destructive. Consider road rage as an example of how destructive and most times dangerous anger can be.

The notion that anger as an emotion is dangerous is not far-fetched. People who express their anger are able to wreak great violence. However, although anger can definitely be abused, it is more than a damaging energy.

Anger is a significant part of our self-defense and self-preservation mechanism. People who don't get angry are not capable of defending and standing up for themselves. This is why anger expressed in a controlled manner is important. Learning how to express their anger correctly, in a healthy and deferential manner is what people need to learn. There are ways that you can express anger without it being uncontrolled and where it affects your health, relationships and your ability to be or remain employed. (Mills, 2019)

At its core, anger is an indication that there is something wrong in your surroundings and attracts your attention. It causes you to act and correct whatever is wrong. When anger is controlled and managed, the feeling of being annoyed, or angry, doesn't impose negative and detrimental health or interpersonal results.

Anger and its Effects

Uncontrolled anger is damaging for both the recipient of the anger as well as the person expressing their anger. People whose anger is uncontrolled alienates and destroys relationships with family, friends and co-workers. Anger that is uncontrolled and makes a person unemployable and impacts negatively on an angry person's emotional and physical health.

Their anger hurts people and then, in the aftermath of one of their fits of anger, wonder why they are shunned, not spoken to or find themselves uninvited to events that they would normally attend. Their anger is destructive to those around them and themselves.

How you are able to handle your anger has very important after-effects for your health and welfare. When you get angry, it activates others to get angry and defensive as well. There is an increase in blood pressure and stress hormones begin to surge. Sometimes, violence occurs. Your anger may give you a name of being a "hot head" that no one will want to be associated with or around.

Aggressive, antagonistic anger can create problems with your health and even early death. It also creates isolation from others which is also a risk factor for grave illness and death. These are just a few reasons that show that learning how to control and properly manage anger is good for you mentally, physically and socially. (Mills, 2019)

Anger and its Psychology

The automatic and natural response to pain, whether emotional or physical is anger. It can happen because a person is ill, has feelings of being rejected, feelings of being endangered or suffer a loss. It doesn't matter what the pain is; what is significant that the pain that has been experienced is not agreeable. Anger never occurs by itself but occurs when it follows feelings of pain. It is considered to be an indirect, secondhand emotion.

By itself, pain is not enough to cause someone to become angry. It happens when there is a combination of pain and anger-generated thoughts. It can be assumptions, evaluations, a misinterpretation, personal assessments that can cause a person to have thoughts of someone trying to hurt them that can be the type of thoughts that can prompt anger. In this sense, it can be considered that anger is a social emotion. (Mills, 2019)

A Substitute Emotion

People cause themselves to be angry so they can avoid feeling pain. People change their feelings of pain to anger because anger feels better than being in pain. This can be done consciously or unconsciously.

There are numerous advantages to be angry rather than in pain. Anger can be a distraction because when people are in pain, they focus on it. The distraction of anger alleviates having to think about pain. Angry people think about a person or people who have caused their pain and have harmed them. This is a shift of the angry person's attention from focusing on their pain. It temporarily guards angry people against having to deal with the real feelings of pain and instead, focuses on getting back at the people they're angry with. Being angry can hide the reality of a situation that can be fear-provoking or that generates feelings of defenselessness. (Mills, 2019)

In addition to affording a good diversion for feeling vulnerable, generating the feeling of anger develops feelings of power, moral superiority and righteousness, not existent when only in pain. The feeling is when you're angry it's with cause and the people who've hurt you should be punished. It's infrequent that a person will get angry with someone who hasn't hurt them in an important way. Anger is only directed at those who have hurt another.

Angry people usually feel that their anger is justified. However, that's not how other people see it and don't agree. There is a social judgment of a person's anger that generates consequences. Although a person who is angry feels justified in acting in an aggressive manner towards another, their contemporaries may not see it in that way. If a person's boss doesn't agree with their anger, it may cost that person their job. If the act of anger was committed illegally, a judge and jury would not see the anger as justified, and the angry person will go to jail. If a husband, wife or significant other doesn't agree that the anger was justified, a marriage or relationship may incur problems, or it could come to an end. (Mills, 2019)

Anger and the Costs and Benefits – Emotional, Social and Health

Justified or not, the feeling of righteousness that a person connects with anger provides a strong, short-term lift to one's self-esteem. A person may feel better feeling anger than to recognize the feelings of pain associated with feeling vulnerable. You can use anger to change the feelings of helplessness and defenselessness to feelings of power and control. Some people transfer all their helpless and vulnerable feelings into anger, so they don't have to deal with them. This transference of feelings is done without they're even realizing that they do this.

Although a person is distracted from feeling helpless or vulnerable, they still feel vulnerable at some level, and anger can't make these feelings disappear. In the end, anger doesn't bring resolution or address the issues that gave the person the feelings of defenselessness and vulnerability but can generate new problems that include health and social issues. (Mills, 2019)

Managing Your Anger

There is help for those who find that they cannot or don't know how to control their anger. That help is found in a program for anger management comprised of procedures to practice and corresponding interventions that are meant to assist angry people to learn the ways of managing their anger and bringing it under control.

Anger management has a number of levels that are implemented to help an angry person better understand where their anger comes from. It begins with a conversation about the cause of anger, the effects of their anger on people's emotional, physical and social well-being.

The anger management techniques will not generate the desired results if only casually used. In order for them to be effective, you must commit to practicing and using them consistently, so their effects have an opportunity to positively affect your life.

Ten Anger Management Tips

- ○ **Think before you speak** – count to ten if you have to first. It's easy to say something regrettable that you can't take back when you're in the heat of an argument. Taking a few moments to think about how you want to express your anger before you speak is a better way to go. Let others who are involved do the same.

- ○ **Express your anger when you feel calm** – once you feel calm enough and can think with a clearer mind, express your irritation in a way that is nonconfrontational, yet assertive. Speak your needs and concerns in a direct and clear manner without harming others' feelings or trying to exert any control over them.

- Exercise – work that anger out of your system. Being physically active helps to decrease stress and anxiety that can cause you to feel angry. Spend time doing physical activities like running, walking or going for a bike ride.

- Timeout – give yourself a timeout, like you would give to your child if it were warranted. Take short breaks at the times of the day that may be more stressful, so you'll be able to handle them better without getting angry or annoyed

- Identify solutions – step back and focus on what it is that makes you angry rather than reacting and blowing up. Is it the mess in your child's bedroom and pushes you over the anger edge? Simple - close the door. Do members of the family have you wait to serve dinner almost every night? Schedule and serve dinner later so everyone can be present. Remember that getting angry isn't the fix of anything and will only make it worse.

- Use humor – anger is like a balloon ready to pop. Let the air out of it instead. Humor can diffuse the tension that goes hand in hand with anger. It also helps you in actually looking at what makes you angry which sometimes can be expectations that are unrealistic. Stay away from sarcasm, that's not humor or humorous. It can also hurt another's feelings and only make things worse

o **Stick with "I" statements** – use the "I" word and avoid placing blame. That will only increase any tension. Be specific and polite. It's better to state that you're upset about a particular situation rather than make your statement in an accusatory manner.

o **No holding grudges** – allowing anger and other negative feelings can push away positive feelings, and they may swallow you up with the feeling of injustice or resentment. However, forgiving someone who has angered you releases the tension of holding on to your anger and both of you can learn from the situation.

o **Practice relaxation** - muscle relaxation and deep breathing can help when your temper begins to boil over. Imagine a tranquil scene, repeat a word or phrase that have a calming effect, listen to soothing music, do yoga, meditate, write a journal. Do whatever it is you need to do to relax.

o **Seek help when needed** – Controlling anger can be a challenge at times for everyone. If you feel you are having a difficult time in managing your temper and your anger outbursts seem to be uncontrolled, and you do things that hurt others, and you later regret, seek help for your anger issues. It will help you to understand why your anger is uncontrolled and you'll be able to get a better grasp on what to do about it.

Chapter 3: Raising Emotional Intelligence

How do you raise your emotional intelligence? For some people, this is not a problem. Actually, for them, it is a characteristic that is innate and instinctive. They have the ability to know their emotions as well as be aware of the emotions of others. For others, not so much. They may be able to have a sense of their own emotions but may not be able to recognize the feelings of others and possibly don't know how.

Emotional intelligence impacts your personal life as well as your performance in the workplace. Understanding and handling your own emotions can step up success and affect your confidence, optimism, and empathy to your social skills, and self-control. Regardless of what profession you are in, whether you manage a large group of people or just yourself, recognizing how effective you are in the control of your emotions, is a great beginning.

Emotional intelligence is not something that is taught. What is it, do you have it, where does it come from, and how important is it?

The ability to learn emotional intelligence is possible. Some tips can help you recognize what emotional intelligence is to find out what level of emotional intelligence you have and attain skills that can be applied in your life every day. (Newman, Martyn, 2019)

We already know that emotional intelligence is how we identify and manage our own emotions and respond to the emotions of others. Our emotions form our thoughts and actions, and it is important to have control of our behavior and establish our competence in managing ourselves effectively. When we develop our emotional conscious, it allows us to attain a deeper knowledge of who we are and give us the ability to have stronger relationships and better communication with others.

This chapter will outline how to raise your emotional intelligence and put it into practice. These suggestions and tips will be beneficial when applied and implemented and become a part of your daily life.

Observe your feelings and how you feel – our lives are hectic jumbles of things to accomplish, errands to run, meetings to attend, day in and out, week after week. With all these activities it is easy to lose track of ourselves, our emotions and how we may, unthinkingly, respond to others. In order to rekindle your connection with your emotions, try setting times over the course of the day to stop and focus on your breathing and your emotions. Take some deep breathes and give attention to where emotion is revealing itself as a feeling that you are having physically. Notice what the sensations feel like. Practice this exercise as often as you can. You will see how it will become natural to interpret how your emotions feel. (Newman, Martyn, 2019)

Attention to your behavior – while you are practicing the observation of your feelings and how it makes you feel physically, give notice to how you behave as well. Notice how you act while experiencing specific emotions, and how they affect you and impact on your life. When we become more aware of how we react to our emotions and our behavior when we experience them, managing them will become easier.

Take time to understand the other side – We sometimes tend to live in a bubble of our own opinion that is usually supported by like-minded people. We don't step out of our comfort zone. It's not a bad idea to find out the viewpoints of the other side and allow your opinions to be challenged, even if you feel your opinion is still the one you wish to maintain. This will help in recognizing and understanding other people's way of thinking and be open to different ideas.

Taking responsibility for your feelings – your emotions come from you, as does how you behave. Taking responsibility for the way you feel and behave, how you express your emotions and demonstrate them by your actions will have an affirmative impact on all parts of your life. (Newman, Martyn, 2019)

Celebrate positive moments – positive emotions are part of emotional intelligence. Reflecting on positive moments and celebrating them help you in having relationships that are satisfying and you generally become more durable. Positive emotions help you move past any adversity you encounter in your relationships.

Recognize the negative as well – negative feelings and reflecting upon them is just as much a part of emotional intelligence as it is to reflect on the positive. When you recognize your negative feelings and why you have those feelings you are becoming a well-rounded person who is able to handle future negative situations.

Breathe – there are moments that life can throw us learning curves and situations that most of us receive a bit of stress regularly. When this happens, we need to manage our emotions and reduce the stress to prevent or minimize any outburst, just breathe. Take a time out – yes, just like a kid, call a time out. Remove yourself from the situation, step outside and breathe in the fresh air, get a drink of water. Keep cool and give you and the situation some space, a moment to get hold of your emotions and a sense of what's happening and thought on how to react and respond.

Emotional intelligence is a process for a lifetime – the process of learning emotional intelligence is developed over time and needs continuous improvement.

Self-Awareness – an important factor of emotional intelligence is self-awareness. It has the ability to identify and understand your own emotions, moods, and character and how they affect other people. An assessment of what you're can do, your weaknesses and strengths, as well as recognizing how others see you. Self-awareness can help to focus on areas that need self-improvement, helping to limit incorrect decisions and better adapt to situations.

Look at yourself objectively – it is not easy to know yourself completely and pretty much impossible to look objectively at oneself as well. Contribution from those who know you are fundamental in your being able to get objective opinions about yourself. Ask questions about what your weaknesses and strengths are and write them down. Compare what is said among the people you ask and check if there is some type of pattern that develops from all their input. This is their objective opinion, so don't argue about their opinions. They may not necessarily be right about their observations, but their opinion is to help you measure your perception of yourself from another person's viewpoint.

What motivates you – when people begin to work on a project, their motivation level is very high. However, keeping the level of motivation high is when difficulty comes into play. There are many times when a project is begun, but not completed because there is a loss of motivation to finish it. Taking the time to know what motivates you and use it to push forward and complete your project.

Log your daily events – one way to be able to accurately assess yourself is to keep a log or a diary by writing down events and situations that happened to you during the day. You can write what the events and situations were, how they made you feel and how you handled them. When you document these details, you become more aware of what you're doing and where problems may be coming from. Over time review what you've made comments on and see if any trends appear in your comments.

Take a break – as noted in the previous chapter on controlling your anger, it states to take a break, meditate, do yoga, read – escape into your own quiet space.
It works wonders for the mind, body and spirit and doesn't hurt.

Recognize what triggers your emotions - individuals who have self-awareness have the ability to acknowledge their emotions while they are occurring. Flexibility with your emotions is crucial as well as adapting them to situations. Don't block your emotions to be seen, but don't be inflexible with them as well. Process your emotions by taking time to process them before you communicate them to others.

Now that you've gotten an outline on how to gauge your emotions, recognize them and manage them, the next way of raising your emotional intelligence is how to recognize the emotions of others.

Empathy is critical in acknowledging the emotions of others and the ability to understand them. Everyone has their own individual set of feelings, triggers, fears, and desires. In order to empathize with others, you're allowing the situations and events they experience resonate with your own in order to respond in suitably.

Empathy is the most important skill to traverse relationships, and it may not come naturally to you, you can learn a few ways to nurture it.

Listen – in order to empathize with others; you need to listen, listen to what they're saying and understand what is being said. *Listening is the core of empathy.* It lets the other person talk without your interrupting them, no preconceptions or skepticism. It's about them, not you. Your own issues are put to the side and paused to be able to absorb and be attentive to their situation and consider their feelings, how and what they feel before you respond or react.

Acknowledge what others are saying - while you're listening to what a person is saying, acknowledging what they are saying by saying "I see" or "I know what you mean" lets the person know that you are listening to them. Nodding your head is also acceptable.

Allow yourself to be approachable – be open to being approachable and accessible, no matter whether you are leading a team, working on another with others, or are a parent.

Be open to others – like being approachable; being open is probably the quickest way to provide an exchange or sign of empathy that is sincere. Listening and connecting to another person's experience with an experience of your own that is similar. Don't have any fear about opening yourself up – it might be the beginning of an enduring relationship.

Their perspective, not yours – you're putting yourself in the other person's shoes by looking at what they're feeling for their perspective. It's the ability to think about how they're feeling from their point of view and switching places with them. There may be no right or wrong about it, but you'll have a better perspective and understanding to be able to give some advice or help resolve an issue.

Social skills – these are referred to as skills needed to effectively handle and affect other people's emotions. It envelops a broad range of abilities, from communicating to dealing with change, building relationships and meeting new people. These are skills that play a part in practically every part of our life, from romantic relationships with our partner to our work life. It is a bit complicated and multifaceted in its complexity and it does need you to use almost every point mentioned. However, here are some other suggestions for you:

Isolate one skill – one way to improve your social skills is to set apart one skill that you want to develop. This gives you the ability to focus on this skill. If you want to be good at this specific skill, spotlight someone who is good at this skill. Watch how they act, and they have their emotions in control, and then apply that knowledge to yourself.

Kick social media to the curb – take your social life off your phone, computer or tablet and get involved with some face-to-face conversations with people will open up a vista you may not have experienced before. You'll develop and gain your social skills from these opportunities. So, instead of texting your best friend about what's going on in your life, invite them out for a drink, or dinner. Emotional intelligence won't develop within the boundaries of un-social media.

What to Avoid

People that have a high EQ rarely exhibit these traits, a good example to follow:

Complaining – it is rare that an emotionally intelligent person feel they are victims, nor do they feel that there is no solution to situations. Instead of blaming others or something, they think and try to find constructive resolutions to resolve the solution privately.

Theatrics and Drama – Emotionally intelligent people listen to others, provide advice, and offer empathy to those who are in need but don't allow the lives of others and their emotions to take effect of their own lives.

Dwelling in the Past – People who have a high emotional intelligence make a choice to learn from the mistakes they've made rather than dwell on the past and relive the negative moments of their lives. They are of the mind to live in the present and look forward to the positive.

Selfishness – there is a certain degree of selfishness in all of us, although there are many levels and degrees. However, to get ahead, a certain amount is necessary, while an overabundance can be destructive to relationships and create disharmony. Consider others' needs and try not to be too selfish

Having emotional intelligence and practicing it each day will help you to be more in tune with yourself and others. By understanding and applying emotional intelligence successfully you will be able to reach your potential and realize your goals.

Chapter 4: Control Your Feelings

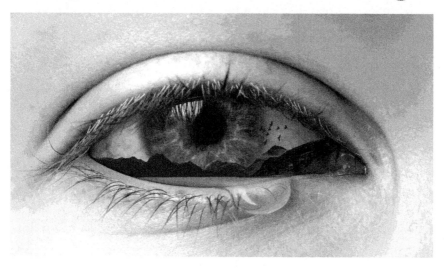

Is it possible to control your emotions?

There are millions of people who unfortunately don't have control of their emotions. The girl who breaks up with her boyfriend because she believed, after he didn't return a couple of phone calls, he was cheating on her. In actuality, he was in a late afternoon meeting that stretched on until mid-evening. Before she finds out the truth, she's left several toxic messages on his voicemail and sent texts as well. Once she finds out the real reason he didn't call, her boyfriend has decided that this is not the type of person he can have a relationship with. The trust factor for him is important, and she lacked the ability to trust him. No matter how much she apologized, he was adamant about his position and ended the relationship.

Or the guy at a crowded bar who gets accidentally brushed by another man as he passes by. As the man turns to offer an apology, the guy decides to punch him in the face telling him to watch where he's walking and lays him flat out on the floor of the bar, disrupting everyone's evening. The aftermath of this uncontrolled emotion is a lawsuit for assault for just a brief accidental brush of one person against another.

Has there been a time when you've said something that you later wished you hadn't and regretted? Does fear get in the way of pursuing an opportunity that could be of benefit? This happens to many people, something that impedes growth or is ruinous to relationships.

When under pressure, some people become extremely emotional. It can be so bad that they make foolish decisions that are regretted after the fact.
When not in control of your emotions, it doesn't just put you in a weak position of being uncontrolled, but it will have you make decisions and take actions that are regrettable later on.

How does one control their feelings? Our emotions are strong and determine your mood, how you interact with others, the amount of money you spend, how you spend your time and how you deal with the trials and challenges you face daily.

When you gain control of your emotions, you become tougher mentally. With knowledge and practice, anyone in need of learning how to do so can get better at managing their emotions. Like with any other skill you learn, regulating your emotions takes dedication and continual practice.

Steps for controlling your emotions

Being in control of your emotions is very much a possibility. Here is how it can be done:

Before making a decision, think sensibly – take the time and think about any decision you may make if time is not of the essence and you have mixed emotions about the situation. Sleeping on it would probably be better. It would give you the time to think things through and have a chance to step back and be more in control of your emotions.

Resist the urge to be impulsive – even if you want to act impulsively, taking control of your emotions is how not to let your emotions rule you but rather you rule them. Don't let your emotions force you to act impulsively. Take your time to think and learn how to react only after using your thought process to make a decision. (Radwant, MSc., M. Farouk, 2017)

Manage your emotions, not stifle them – Managing your emotions is not the same as stifling or suppressing them. If you feel pain or are sad about a situation, you shouldn't ignore these emotions. They don't go away. Addressing them is the best you can do so that, eventually, they do become manageable and go away.

If ignored, your emotional wounds can become worse. Stifling your emotions can cause you to use coping skills that are unhealthy, like alcohol, drugs or food. Realize that recognizing your emotions don't have to control you when you acknowledge them, which is an important factor in gaining control of your feelings. You may become angry for some reason yet make a choice to be calm and focused on being calm instead.

There are ways to gain control of your emotions that will benefit the way you feel as well as how others around you will feel as well. (Morin, 2018)

Naming your emotions – when you become emotional and before you change how you're feeling, acknowledging what you're facing at the moment. Is your emotion one of sadness, are you nervous, has an occurrence made you feel disappointed, or a person or event made you angry?

Remember that, as you read you read in a previous chapter, anger is a substitute emotion to hide vulnerable feelings, like embarrassment, pain or shame. Keep this in mind and pay attention to what's actually going on with your feelings.

Give your emotions a name. You may feel a number of emotions all at once, like sadness, frustration, and anxiety. When you label how you feel, it takes the bite out of the emotion. It can help you take note of how your decisions will be impacted on by the way you feel. (Morin, 2018)

Restructure your thoughts – the way you recognize events is how it affects your emotions. If you're feeling apprehensive and then called into the human resources office, you may think that you're going to be let go from your job. If you're feeling upbeat and happy and you get the same request from human resources, you may think you're getting that transfer to the Paris branch of your company that you and applied for and it's going to be offered to you.

Think about how your emotions are affecting how you're looking at situations. Restructure your thoughts to create a more realistic view. If you've been invited to an event where you can network and meet new people, but think you'd rather not go because all the negative thoughts of no one talking to you, or you don't think you have anything to talk about with others, take a pause and restructure those thoughts. Think about how meeting new people by introducing yourself will give you the ability to learn about them.

Pausing and taking a step back is one of the easiest ways to get a different viewpoint. You can think about what you would say to someone who has the same problem. When you answer that question, it will ease some of the emotion you had been feeling out of the equation, allowing you to think more sensibly.

Change your thought process if you find that you are dwelling too much on negative things. Do something physical, like cleaning your bathroom, emptying out that "catch-all" drawer or going for a walk can help you stop that negative pondering.

Boost your mood up – here are some examples of ways to boost your mood when the one you're in is bad and irritating to you and others. You can

- Go for a walk – the air is fresh, and it will invigorate you mentally and physically. While you're on that walk, why not listen to your favorite uplifting music. Music is always a mood enhancer, and the more upbeat, the better.
- If you can, meditate for 20 minutes. Light a candle to include aromatherapy to the mix and by the time your meditation has ended, you're out of your funk.

o Get together with friends and talk about uplifting things –
the next baseball team coming to town to play against your
home team, the upcoming sale at your favorite shop in
town and the items you're hoping to purchase at bargain
prices.

Boosting your mood is so much better than isolating yourself,
complaining to everyone around you and falling deeper into a
bad mood. (Morin, 2018)

Are your emotions controlling you? – *Life is 10% what
happens to you and 90% on how you react to it - Charles R.
Swindoll*

Regulating your emotions – Your feelings can't be mastered,
but you can learn that they can be regulated. Your emotional
response goes through many stages. Depending on your
preparation, you can either have a controlled, wise-minded
response, or emotions that can act out like a runaway train. You
want to prepare for your response before a situation arises.

Managing Negative Emotions at Work

Having negative emotions while at your workplace is not the
ideal situation. Even if you are the boss, it's not a reason to
impose your negative feelings on others at the job. For one, it
doesn't boost morale, but rather demoralizes your team and is

not a positive motivator for your staff. Secondly, it doesn't do well for your management to see or hear that your bad moods are creating a toxic work environment. If good people are lost to other companies because of your inability to create a positive, thriving environment, you can be the next person your company loses, and not by your choice.

Continue to Practice Your Regulating Skills – Managing emotions can be hard at times, and there could be a bit of emotional anger that at times will flare up and get the best of you.

The more attention and time you take in regulating your emotions, you will become mentally stronger. Your confidence will soar when you begin to see the changes and your ability to handle those moments of emotional discomfort. You'll also recognize that you have the ability to make choices that are healthy that will alter your mood.

Chapter 5: Self-Discipline and You

How many times have you begun a diet, started a home project, or said to yourself you want to begin a regime of getting in shape by going to the gym? You begin that diet, the home project and make it to the gym. You set goals, sometimes too lofty to achieve and then, something interrupts that flow of activity. You cheat on the diet, once, then twice, then three times and the diet falls to the wayside. That project was more than you expected and was cutting into your weekends and other activities you wanted to do, so you decide you'll hire someone to complete the project. And the gym? You tried getting up early to go but just couldn't make it out of bed and then, you tried to make it after work, but there were some evenings where you had to work overtime, and the other evenings – well you were just too tired after a long day to get there. What about the weekends? There were the outings with the family, the kids had their softball or soccer games, or there were dance and music classes they needed to be chauffeured to, so that lets you off the hook for the weekend.

So what happened to the commitments you made? Where was the self-discipline? At the core of anyone who is successful in their achievements is self-discipline. It can be a success in your personal life like the diet, the home project, or getting to the gym, or in your business life, any success you desire to achieve begins with the ability to control yourself through discipline. Every thought, behavior, emotion, and habit that you have needs to be disciplined.

There is no personal success, goal or accomplishment that can be realized without self-discipline. It is the singular most important characteristic that is needed to accomplish any personal excellence of any kind.

Self-discipline is the ability to control your feelings and conquer your weaknesses; the ability to go after what one thinks is right regardless of the temptation to desert it (Merriam-Webster, 2019)

You need to understand how disciplining yourself is an important ingredient to being successful. However, self-discipline is and has been a matter of discussion for many years and is not something new. Many successful people are supporters of self-discipline. You need to be able to make decisions, take action and implement your plan irrespective of discomfort, difficulties or obstacles that may get in your way.

Successful people understand that the way to achieve their goals is through discipline, how to use it by developing a basis of beneficial habits that has aided them to see things through.

Self-discipline is something you can learn, but you are probably asking how it is formed or developed? What is it that makes one person successful in having control over their actions, thoughts and behavior, and others to fail? Why are some people conscious and conscientious in what they do daily, and others kind of throw it against the proverbial wall to see what will stick?

Habits are the answer to these questions. Realize that 40% of the behavior we exhibit is driven by habit. If you want to be self-disciplined, your habits are what you have to control. If you have bad habits or are lacking in habits that would be beneficial in your quest for self-discipline, then this chapter will lay out the habits you need to succeed.

Being self-disciplined doesn't mean being restrictive in living your life and giving up all the things you enjoy or not being able to have fun and relax. What it does mean is to learn about focusing on your goals and persist in accomplishing that goal. Developing a mindset where you are governed by your own planned choices rather than run by your bad habits, emotions or the influence of others. (Hereford, 2019)

Some habits can help you to learn to discipline yourself. If you can integrate these habits into your daily life, you can develop a foundation that will help you achieve your goals.

Developing Self-Discipline

It takes time to begin to develop self-discipline. You will become stronger the more time you put towards training and building your discipline. If you do too much when you exercise, the possibility of injuring yourself is great. It is the same with building self-discipline. You need to take one step at a time and not overdo or be disappointed in yourself if you set the goals too high in the beginning. Begin with the decision to proceed forward and learn what it takes to get there.

What are your bad triggers and what motivates you

Acknowledging that you have cravings and urges will help you identify the areas where your ability to resist temptation is low and how to side-step those situations. This is the first step in getting to know yourself and your triggers, especially bad ones. If you can't resist certain foods like potato chips, cookies, French fries or other temptations, don't have them around and stay away from them. Having them around will only lure you into eating them in your weak moments. Additionally, if you know that being pressured isn't how you best perform and doesn't work for you, establish an environment that encourages you to build self-discipline instead of having the process disrupted. Eliminate any temptations and bolster yourself with encouraging and soothing objects and items such as motivational slogans and photos of what you want to accomplish. (Hereford, 2019)

Get Organized

In order to get self-disciplined and work towards your goals, you need to be organized. Being organized is a habit that you need to apply not only to your personal life but professional life as well. This is an overall organization, including all things in your home and office, as well as organizing your mind.

When you are organized, you are disciplined. If you're completely scattered, with everything all over the place, you need to start small. Begin by organizing one small area each day. So, if your desk drawers are a mess, take one drawer at a time and organize it. Once your desk is done, move on and organize a closet, color-coding your wardrobe, matching your shoes in pairs, etc. Organize a space each day. One small thing a day and you'll see and feel a difference.

As in other habits, being organized as a habit can build up over time. It does need to have some attention and effort, but in the end, the payoff is tremendous. When the physical space around you is organized, your mind settles into feeling less stress and being more relaxed and ready to focus more clearly.

Once you are more organized in your life, you can be more self-disciplined. Along with organizing your desk drawers or your closet, you should have a list of how each drawer or closet is organized. When you use something and are finished using it, return it to its proper place. Being aware of keeping organized impacts on our life. The little things are what you need to pay attention to and doing so will realize tremendous benefits. (Kanaat, Robert, 2018)

Some behaviors should become routine

When you decide what goals are important to you and you endeavor to work towards them, establish a routine that you keep daily that will aid you to achieve those goals. For example, if you want to lose weight and make a commitment to eat right and exercise every day and work this into your daily schedule and part of building your self-discipline. Also, eliminate any bad habits that can be self-defeating, like having any cookies or potato chips stored in the pantry and sneak-eating. This type of behavior can put you in a bad state of mind because you cheated on your weight loss program and gets in the way of your positive thoughts and self-discipline. Having a bad habit can also be perceived as a bad habit. (Hereford, 2019)

Manage your time

When you manage your time correctly, you have the ability to have time for things that matter. In other words, there's an opportunity for activities that we have in place to aid us in achieving our goals. If we want to achieve our long-term goals, there are actions that we have to perform that may not be crucial but carry an amount of importance.

Quadrant 2 is known the Important but Not Urgent quadrant of activities in time management, but most people spend time in Quadrant 4, the Not Important and Not Urgent activities. These are time wasters. (Kanaat, Robert, 2018)

How we effectively manage our time is how we have the capability to be self-disciplined. Some of the most successful people in their areas are well-known time managers of the world because they use time as an advantage rather than a detractor.

Time Management Quadrants

Manage -1 Short-Term Crises & Problems Important & Urgent	Focus - 2 On Long-Term Goals Important But Not Urgent
Avoid-3 Interruptions & Distractions Urgent But Not Important	Limit - 4 Time-Wasting Activities Not Impotant & Not Urgent

Persistence and Determination

There is no way a set of habits that will help you in becoming self-disciplined would be complete without being persistent and following up with determination. Being persistent and having determination is what helps us not give up. It helps us to get back up and try again even when we fail. Self-discipline would be pretty much impossible to develop if we don't have persistence and determination.

Why do we need to have these habits? Frankly, accomplishing what we make a commitment to achieve is not easy. Being frustrated, getting discouraged and giving up is easy. It takes much less effort to give up than it does to keep on and continuing to drive through, especially if what we are working towards has pain attached to it, and it's what we have to go through before we finally reach our goal and extract any pleasure for reaching it. (Kanaat, Robert, 2018)

Exercise or participate in activities

Participating in sports is an exceptional way to augment self-discipline. The training has you setting goals, focusing on your emotional and mental energies, get physically fit, learn to work as part of a team and get to know other people and get along with them. You learn to work hard and make every effort to do your best. This teaches you to incorporate the same thought methods and disciplines into your life.

Another way to practice self-discipline is to learn how to play a musical instrument. The repetition, the focus, and application that is needed in learning how to play an instrument is inestimable. It programs your mind to choose what is right rather than easy when you achieve self-discipline in any one area of your life.

Self-Denial

In order to build your self-discipline, you need to learn how to say no to some of your, urges, impulses and feelings. Even if you don't feel like you want to do it, coach yourself to do what's right. Instead of having some kind of snack every day, skip having that snap to only once or twice a week. Read more and limit watching TV. Take a step back, a deep breath, think before you act and refrain from yelling at someone who has irritated you. Before you yell, give thought to the result of what your yelling will begin, or end. Practicing self-denial and self-restraint aid in developing the habit of keeping things, and yourself, under control. (Hereford, 2019)

Be inspired by those you admire

One of the best stories that should inspire anyone is about Michael Jordan and his great achievements as a basketball player. His achievement to being one of the greatest basketball players of all time came from his determination, persistence, and willingness to work hard at his craft and technique as it did on his tremendous talent. He was focused on what he wanted and though his desire and discipline became one of the best players ever. It worked for him, and it could definitely work for anyone.

Envision your rewards

Accomplishing your goals is one of the most rewarding feelings one can have. There is a technique that top athletes and successful achievers do and that is to protect yourself into the future. Envision the outcome that you want. Feel how gratifying is and realize the benefits you will relish. Don't forget what it takes to get there. (Hereford, 2019)

The Benefits of Self-Discipline

Self-discipline builds self-confidence. When you are self-disciplined, you are able to accomplish more and you're more productive. The levels of frustration, obstacles, and emotions that are negative are better managed and you are able to maintain a higher tolerance and positive attitude.

When you're self-disciplined, you establish a good work ethic, your health is better, and your finances are more stable. You have the ability to reach the most difficult goals you are striving for more efficiently. (Hereford, 2019)

In order to be the controllers of our life and destiny, self-control and self-discipline is something we must develop. Working towards and focusing on long-term goals and its benefits rather than on the discomfort of the short-term we can embolden ourselves to develop self-discipline.

The more disciplined you become, the easier your life will get.

Chapter 6: The Key to A Great Relationship

What is the key to a great relationship? Some people think it's communication, while others think it's respect. Yet others believe that it's honesty and trust. Actually, it's all these things and more.

Relationships are, at best, great to have especially with someone you like, not just love, and at worse, something that one would probably want to be as far away as possible from and have it ended.

When we see an elderly couple who are still engaged with one another, walking and talking, holding hands, or sitting together laughing and sharing a joke or funny story, it may give you a feeling of warmth and a bit of wonderment as well. How did they do it? How have they been together all these years and continue to enjoy one another? Why can they have such a warm and loving relationship when there are people who start out as couples with all good intentions and can't make it past the year mark, some staying together in even less time than that.

Some people instinctively know that they're just not into each other, or at least, one of the two know that their relationship won't last and end the relationship because, for them, it just won't work out. Then other relationships end as soon as there is a problem, not taking the time to try to work out the issue. The relationship was "perfect" until an imperfection comes along, and they didn't know how or didn't want to work things out.

Relationships are not perfect, because no one is perfect. But what they are and what they can be are the joining of people who are willing to share an open, honest, trusting and, at times, humorous relationship, who cares enough, respect each other enough and *choose* to have as great a relationship as they can.

Life is colorful and relationships add to the color. In order to have happy, strong and meaningful relationships, we have to realize that being honest, communicative, respectful, understanding, and throwing in humor are the ingredients that can be to a great relationship.

Our relationship with our partner is probably the most important of our relationships because everything comes from a good personal relationship. If you have children, they benefit from your having a strong, loving relationship. So do other family members, your friends and your All of these characteristics can apply to any of our relationships so they can all be great:

Communication - is an important factor in having a good relationship. You can't have a thriving relationship without openly communicating with one another. If there's a problem, like you don't want to go to an event and would rather spend your time together going out to dinner and spending some one-on-one time, you need to state how you feel. This is not to start an argument, or to be disagreeable, but what you'll need to communicate that you'd rather spend time with just them, alone. Your partner won't know how you feel unless you say something. They don't have a crystal ball or mind read how you feel. It's better than going to the event and feeling resentful that you're not spending time alone with your partner. (Cygert, 2017)

When you don't speak up and talk about your wants, needs, desires and keep your feelings to yourself, you're not nurturing a healthy, open relationship. Holding resentments, or misinterpreted discussions inside and then one day blow up at your unsuspecting partner can be extremely damaging to your relationship.

Speak up, communicate to encourage and nurture a healthy, open and honest relationship. It's unfair not to do so and for only one person be accommodating to the other. A relationship cannot flourish without communicating with one another so speak your mind and accept your thoughts.

Honesty and Trust – in order for a relationship to be strong and successful it is vital that there is honesty and trust of one another. Being honest with your partner will give them no reason to distrust you or them. You can accept almost anything in a relationship, but if there's dishonesty, it is hurtful and casts a cloud over the relationship.

Honesty and trust are not to make a relationship rigid or that you can't be an individual in a partnership. Just be honest about whatever you're doing because keeping your actions hidden or they hiding something from you that later comes outcasts doubt and mistrust on the relationship.

If you try to build or maintain a relationship where one partner is dishonest, it's like building a house made of sand. The mistrust will always have one partner questioning the other partner's motives or actions, and the partner that was dishonest and is trying to regain the trust becomes frustrated at constantly being questioned or second-guessed. Dishonesty brings nothing but negativity into a relationship. Being dishonest and betraying a trust can be destructive to a relationship and sometimes, brings the relationship to an end when trust is broken. (Cygert, 2017)

Learn to Forgive – people are not mistake-proof. They make mistakes all the time, and that includes in their relationships as well. Some things are unforgivable in a relationship. Cheating, for many, is unforgivable because it signals that the other person and the relationship didn't have any value to the person who cheated. However, unless it is extreme, most anything else can be forgiven. Forgiveness is necessary for a relationship because neither person is perfect. If your partner comes home from work disgruntled because a presentation to a client didn't go well, snaps at you when you ask how was their day, barely speaks to you during dinner and has a foul disposition all through the rest of the evening, give them some space and let them come around when their ready. They'll more than likely realize they've made a mistake by taking their anger out on you, tell you about their bad day and the presentation that didn't go well and apologize. And that's when you tell your partner they're forgiven. It's simple, yet sometimes a difficult place to get to. Understanding, patience and care play a large role in these instances that relationships go through, and in the end, it strengthens a relationship.

Appreciate and Respect One Another – there isn't love in a relationship if appreciation and respect for your partner, and they of you, is not present and not expressed. A relationship that promotes and supports one another and demonstrates respect and appreciation is the foundation of a healthy relationship. The way to show respect and appreciation is to be willing to navigate a compromise, be considerate, respect boundaries, speak respectfully, even when you argue (no name calling or the use of profanity) and being protective of your partners. Also, make sure that your partner is respecting you by acknowledging your worth, acting ethically, being a person of your word, setting boundaries and expect them to be honored, and showing that you have respect for yourself. Show appreciation for your partner, accepting who they are, the support you receive from them, all the big and little things they do for you, and how they make you feel like an equal and an individual when they promote your building your own identity.

Humor – Laugh Every Day – when you share a joke or funny story with your partner, it brightens up the day. It is very important to share a laugh. You're sharing your experiences and life with a partner that you care for and enjoy having fun with. It's healthy to joke and laugh with one another. It sometimes even lightens the mood when you're having a tiff over something that, in the scope of things, is small and inconsequential. When you and your partner begin to realize how ridiculous it is to argue about something and begin to joke about how silly it all is, humor can bring it to an end. It's no fun being serious all the time. It's more fun having a laugh with your partner, keeping the relationship upbeat and alive with humor with daily laughter and seeing a happy smile on their face. (Cygert, 2017)

Giving and Getting Emotional Support – in a relationship, it's necessary to exhibit emotional support for your partner. Men may come across as stoic and unaffected by an emotional event, but don't be fooled. They are feeling emotions and just display it in a different way than a woman does. Whatever the case, we all have emotions and supporting each other when there is a need to, whether it's struggling with the sadness of the loss of a parent, close family member, or a life-long friend, or whatever the reason may be, emotional support for someone who you care about is how you show empathy and understanding for them. Emotional downturns take time to heal, but with love and support from a partner, it will help it to pass.

Don't Forget the Small Things – there's magic in the small things we do for each other in a relationship. Actually, those small gestures, like a funny greeting card you stick in your partner's briefcase so they can get a surprise and have a laugh while at work is a loving gesture. Or when your partner prepares your favorite Sunday breakfast because you've had a busier than usual week can make your week. The small things are really appreciated and the memories that stand out more than you realize. There's something really special in doing the small things that make a relationship special. Knowing that your partner feels valued and happy is an uplifting feeling. Don't forget the small things – they're much bigger than you can imagine.

Rejoice in the Achievements – Your happiness for your own achievements should be the same for your partner's accomplishments. Showing happiness for your partner when they've achieved their goals gives your partner a true sense of how happy you for them and in accomplishing their goals. Showing your pride for what your partner has achieved will bring you and your partner closer together and strengthen the relationship.

Share Your Interests – you don't have to accommodate your partner if you have interests in common that you can share with one another. There will probably be times when you won't want to do the same thing and compromising on an activity will help you meet in the middle on what you want to do. But having interests that you can share, like bike riding or playing golf lets the two of you have an activity that you enjoy sharing with each other and that you can do together. It's great to be able to converse about something the both of you like, and it can be even more interesting talking about some things you don't agree on that can make for good conversation as well.

Love – is a wonderful feeling to have for another person. If you don't have love, you pretty much miss life. Love is a gift that life gives you and even if you're successful, happy, and wealthy, it really doesn't mean anything if there's no one in your life to share it with. Love can join people to build a loving life together that some people would want to have. Yet, sometimes a healthy and flourishing relationship cannot be sustained by love alone. That can be because the partners are really different from each other, the relationship isn't an easy one, and only one of the partners may want to put in the effort to maintain the relationship. All in all, a relationship without love is not a healthy relationship. Let your partner know how you feel about them, show them affection and make it a priority to have time just for the two of you. All the physical intimacy can contribute to making a relationship healthy, but if love is missing, it doesn't mean anything at all. (Cygert, 2017)

There isn't a relationship that doesn't have its peaks and valleys and bumps in the road, but a strong relationship can get through those times of struggle. Take the time to do a health check of your relationship by going over these points on how to have a great relationship. Bolster the positive and work on the negative so your relationship is as natural, healthy and loving it can be. Keep your love alive!

Chapter 7: Communications Skills in The Workplace

If there is one place that cohesive, clear and precise communication is needed, it's in the workplace. So many decisions hinge on what is communicated within an organization – staff to team leader, team leaders to upper management, management to owners or CEOs and communication to a company's client.

Communication is the core of any business. Deals can be made with clear, concise and logical communication, or broken because of an unclear, muddled miscommunication. And the manner of how something is communicated is just as important.

Communicating effectively with superiors, associates and staff is indispensable no matter what type of industry someone is employed. People who are working in the digital age must have the knowledge of how to successfully send and receive messages via email, phone, social media and in person. If you have good communication skills, they will benefit you throughout your career, help you in getting hired for a position, and lead to subsequent promotions. (The Balance Careers, 2019)

Workplace communication is the method of information being exchanged in verbal and non-verbal within an organization. There are many avenues of communication in the workplace. In order to be a valuable and effective member of your organization, it is critical that you are skilled in all the various methods and means of communication that your organization uses and deem appropriate.
(Skill Builder LMS, 2017)

The organizational objective needs to be achieved by effective communication in the workplace. Communication is extremely important to organizations because it boosts efficiency and productivity. When there is communication that is ineffective between employees there, it causes wasted time, confusion, and decreases the organization's productivity. Effective communication between staff members can prevent misunderstandings that may cause friction.

Communication needs to pass from sender to receiver. This has to happen regardless of the method of communication.

Communication can be effective if it is understood by the receiver and there can be a response in return. All types of communication include listening, speaking, reading, and skills involving reasoning.

When a communication passes from the originator to the receiver, the opportunity for the original meaning of the message to change is quite possible. Listening, reasoning and feedback is a critical part of the procedure, as it is a chance for the sender to ensure the receiver understood the message.

The Importance of Effective Communication - there are three important points associated with effective workplace communication:

- o There is an improvement in productivity with workplace communication

- Employee job satisfaction increases with workplace communication

- A positive effect on turnover rates and absenteeism is seen with workplace communication

Communication in the Workplace – this should happen in a way that has a positive response to individual differences. Think of the following:

- Treat all individual with respect, sensitivity, and courtesy and value them

- Cultural differences should be recognized

- Develop and support trust, confidence and positive relationships with constructive communication

- Use basic tactics to overcome any barriers in communication

How you communicate effects your ability to be compatible and work well with people and get the tasks that you want or need to be done. Communication can be conveyed in positive and negative ways regardless of whether it's verbal, written or visual.

People need to get feedback on how others may perceive or decipher how they are communicating and find out how they're communicating and whether it needs improvement or is it misunderstood. There are times our communication may be perceived as dictatorial or aggressive although that was never the intention.

Verbal Communications

When we verbally communicate, we should speak clearly and *listen* carefully making sure what was said is understood. If you need clarification of the meaning of the information, confirm the meaning by asking questions to avoid any miscommunication and misunderstanding.

One of the best was to be a good communicator is to be a good listener. There isn't anyone who likes communicating with a person who only cares about talking about her two cents and doesn't extend the courtesy of listening to the other person.

Not being a good listener will make it hard to understand what you're being asked to do. It would be a good idea to practice active listening. How you practice is to listen very carefully to what another person is saying, ask questions to clarify the message and intent, rephrase what the person is saying to make sure there is an understanding. Active listening allows you to better comprehend what the other person is saying and can properly respond. (The Balance Careers, 2019)

Allow for others to speak. Conversations are a two-way event. If there is a difficult conversation, involve yourself in it when it's necessary. Avoiding a difficult conversation by not saying anything can usually make things worse. And check the tone that you use is one that is open and non-confrontational and encourages feedback. (Skill Builder LMS, 2017)

Clarity and Conciseness

Saying just what you want to say and being brief is another way to exhibit good verbal communication. You're not talking too much or too little. This means to state your message in just a few words, clearly, precisely and distinctly whether you're on the phone, or in an email. If you speak in a jumbled, rambling manner, you'll possibly be tuned out by the listener, or they will not be sure what you want.

Sociability and Friendliness

It's important to have a polite and nice demeanor with your coworkers in the workplace. This is significant in both written as well as face-to-face communication. When you exhibit a friendly tone, or simply smile, you can persuade your coworkers to engage in honest and open communication with you. Personalizing an email or a note at the beginning of an email to your coworkers or staff can make the receiver of the email feel appreciated.

Self-Confidence

When you're interacting with others, it's vital that you exhibit self-confidence. Confidence lets your coworkers know that you have certainty in what you're saying. Displaying confidence can be done by making eye contact or having a firm but friendly tone of voice. Don't make your statements sound like you're asking a question. Don't act or sound aggressive or arrogant. These are two traits that are not welcomed in the workplace. Always listen and empathize with the other person.

Empathy

Being empathetic to others by saying "I understand how you feel" and putting yourself in their position will exhibit that you are listening to the other person and respecting their viewpoints. Important to note – even if you may disagree with a team leader, manager, coworker or staff member, it is critical to respect and understand their opinion and point of view.

Having an Open Mind

A good communicator is open to listening and comprehending the other person's viewpoint instead of getting your own message across. When you're willing to enter into a dialogue, and entering a conversation with flexibility, even with someone with whom you disagree, you will have more constructive and honest conversations.

Nonverbal Communication

The message that you convey is colored by your eye contact, body language, hand motion and voice tones. An open posture that is relaxed (arms open, not crossed and legs relaxed) and a calm, friendly tone will give you the appearance of being accessible and encourages others to speak with you openly.

Your eye contact is important in communicating with others. When you look at a person you are making eye contact with; you want to exhibit that you're focused on them and the conversation, you are engaged and attentive. However, don't stare at the person. This may make them feel uncomfortable.

While you're talking, notice the nonverbal signals that you're receiving from the other person. As an example, if the person is avoiding making direct eye contact with you, they may be feeling uncomfortable or possibly concealing the truth.

(The Balance Careers, 2019)

Communicating via Email and Other Written Communications

When reviewing an email, read and then re-read the email before sending it out. Make sure the grammar, tone, and spelling are correct before it's read by others. Make sure the subject of the email is pertinent and has a subject heading that corresponds with the content of the email. Contact information should be clear and available for those who read the email can contact the author if necessary. Write emails that are professional and polite, concise, using well-founded points and doesn't have lengthy unnecessary, inconsequential ramblings. Avoid copying anyone on the email that has no relevant connection to the topic or content. Also, an extremely important point is *not to discuss confidential information in an email. Ever.*

There is a professional environment in the workplace that means every kind of communication that is written as a professional standard that is expected. The expectation that all communication that is written

- o Is easy to understand

- o Avoids unnecessary repetition, gets to the point and isn't written with sentences that are long, jumbled or muddled and rambling

- o Do not use slang, sexist or racist language, or language that is discriminatory or offensive. A sure way to be terminated

- o Don't write in an onslaught of technical terminology. Unless it is necessary for the purpose of the email specifically requiring technical terms, plain, simple English will suffice.

Being Respectful

People will want to have open communications with you when you exhibit that you have respect for them and their ideas.

Remembering a person's name and greeting them personally, listening to them when they are speaking, and making eye contact makes a person feel recognized, respected and appreciated. When you're speaking on the phone, remain focused on the conversation and prevent distractions.

When you send an email, you can convey respect by reviewing and editing your message. Sending an email that is written in a sloppy and jumbled manner will confuse the recipient. They will probably feel that you don't respect them enough to process and think out your content and communication to them.
(The Balance Careers, 2019)

Giving Feedback

You may be called upon to give and/or receive feedback. Being able to do so is a skill that is very important in order to be viewed as a way of bolstering morale or showing appreciation for someone's performance in the workplace. Supervisors and managers should always provide their staff with feedback that is constructive and empowering. Whether it be by a weekly status report, email or phone, if an employee is doing a good job, or you thank them for the efforts they put into producing the final product of a report or a presentation, praising them is a great motivator for them to continue to thrive in their position.

Conversely, be open and accepting of feedback from others. Listen to what, if any, issues are being told to you, ask questions to clarify any portion of the information you are unsure of and endeavor to implement the feedback you receive. If it's praise for your performance in the workplace, remember to thank them and let them know their praise is appreciated. (The Balance Careers, 2019)

Choosing the Right Form of Communication

Understanding what form of communication that you need to use and apply to certain situations is an important communication skill. As an example, there is going to be a review of the salaries of some staff members, or there are going to be layoffs from one of the company's departments. This type of communication should be done one-on-one in person.

There may be an issue you need to relay to a particular person in management who is the only person that can address the issue and correct it. However, they're pretty busy, so an email will probably be the best way to communicate with them. The person will appreciate that you recognize their busy schedule and get back to you positively and in a timely manner. (The Balance Careers, 2019)

Ways of Communicating to Avoid

During the course of a busy workday, there may be ways of communicating that are really not acceptable to use.

- o Don't talk about personal issues when communicating with others who you have a friendship in the workplace. Save those conversations and/or emails AND texting for your lunch break or after business hours. The company computer shouldn't be used for your personal email life. Planning a camping trip with your work buddy? Save that communication to do on your own time.

- o Don't yell across an office floor. Politely walk over to the other person's office or cubicle to speak with them. It's disturbing to others and frankly, downright rude.

- o Don't put your call on speaker unless you have your own office and can close the door. It's disturbing to others working around you who may be trying to concentrate on writing a report or may be on the phone themselves with a vendor or a client. Be considerate of your coworkers.

- o Don't gossip. This is a form of communication that is a time waster and is counterproductive to maintaining a harmonious work environment. This is not to say that a workplace should be perfect because it can never be when inhabited by people. It is to say that gossiping, backbiting or being uncooperative with other people is immature and doesn't belong in the workplace. The workplace is for professionals. Communicate and treat one another accordingly.

Communicating with Customers and Clients

You provide a service, sell a product or finish a job for a customer or client outside your company. Conveying a respectful and polite demeanor when using both verbal and non-verbal communications to reply to a customer or client request appropriately is extremely important.

There are times that miscommunication can happen in numerous ways and can develop problems in the workplace. What is heard by your customer or client can be misinterpreted and miscommunication can occur. (Skill Builder LMS, 2017)

- How you phrase what your saying can be misinterpreted
- Body language that doesn't line up with your words can be confusing in communicating with a customer or client
- The customer or client may not be focusing on what you're saying, or you are not listening to them properly

Here are ways to aid your communication skills effectively when interacting with customers and clients:

Speak concisely and clearly. Don't rush your words and speak at a rate that can be understood to provide the correct information

Acknowledge the customer by their name – this gives the customer the feeling of being valued and special

Acknowledge non-verbal messages. Display positive and fitting body language at all times.

Don't be judgmental. Don't judge the way a customer presents themselves or how they're dressed. Be open and have an open stance and a congenial tone.

Always be professional and respectful of a customer's feelings. Be aware of your words and tone.

Show interest in people and take a real interest in a customer's needs. This builds trust and a positive relationship with the customer.

Ask questions and be accepting of feedback. Ask your customers questions that are open-ended to find out what they are exactly seeking. (Skill Builder LMS, 2017)

The workplace is a professional environment that you spend quite a bit of time in on a weekly basis. Communicating with your coworkers, management, customers and clients is extremely important for you to learn and understand. As you grow in your professional life, your mastery of communicating in your profession will help you on both a personal and business level. Implementing these communication guidelines correctly will surely get you noticed.

Chapter 8: Boosting Emotional Intelligence

How do you increase your emotional intelligence? Today, this ongoing trend of getting in touch with your "EQ" had been receiving more attention and it is no fad. There have been thousands of studies that have demonstrated the power of EQ assessments in relation to leadership potential, job performance and whether someone is employable. It's also important to note that emotional intelligence has been emphasized even beyond the workplace. Higher scores have been linked to success in relationships, as well as physical and mental health and happiness.

This is great news for people with high emotional intelligence scores. But what can those whose scores are lower do to improve their self-awareness as well as their interpersonal skills? Emotional intelligence is a mixture of personality traits. Nothing is set in stone and is shaped by our experiences from our childhood and relatively stable over time.

Sculpting emotionally intelligent behaviors means that you need to dedicate time and to focus in order to attain it. This is also true when helping others to act with emotional intelligence when it's not in their nature to do so. (Chamorro-Premuzic, 2017)

There are several ways to boost your emotional intelligence.

Instead of self-deception be self-aware

Our personality and emotional intelligence are a combination of two parts – our identity, which is how we see ourselves and reputation which is how others see us. When we attain real self-awareness, we are realizing and achieving a realistic view of our strengths and weaknesses and how these traits compare with others'.

For example, there are those people who rate their own emotional intelligence as high, yet only a small group of those same people will be given ratings of being emotionally intelligent by others. You won't be able to turn self-deception into self-awareness without receiving accurate feedback, the kind that comes from assessments that are data-based like a valid personality test or 360-degree feedback surveys. These tests are the basis to help discover any blind spots that are emotional intelligence related only because other people are usually too polite to give us negative feedback. (Chamorro-Premuzic, 2017)

Consider your own emotions

Think about your own use of emotions. Here are a few examples of thinking about how you normally react when:

- o An email pops up at the office and indicates you mishandled an assignment
- o Your partner blames you for a situation and you feel the blame is unfair
- o You're cut off by another driver on your way home from work
- o An associate begins to cry without provocation

By reviewing each example and identifying how you honestly would react in each instance helps you be become more aware and begin the process of building your self-control. (Bariso, 2016)

Use the internal pause button

The pause button can be as simple as taking a step back or a deep breath while you stop and think before you speak or act. It's wishful thinking, but imagine if everyone practiced pressing that internal pause button. Emails would be shorter; meetings wouldn't drag on because someone needs to talk on and on, and how the many provocative, incendiary comments that are bandied on social media could be eliminated. However, pausing, in theory, is simple yet it's hard to put into practice.

A bad or a stress-filled day can prevent the ability to practice pausing even if we're relatively good at managing our emotions. When you practice pausing before taking action or speaking, you develop the habit of thinking first.

Make self-focus into other-focus

Paying attention to others is critical to career success. However, for those with lower levels of emotional intelligence find it difficult to see things from other people's viewpoints, particularly when there is no right or wrong. In order to develop an other-focus, it begins with basic recognition and appreciation of another person's strengths, weaknesses, and beliefs. Brief discussions will lead to a better understanding of how to influence and motivate others.

Be rewarding to deal with

People who are successful and more employable are inclined to be viewed as rewarding to deal with. People who are rewarding to deal with are inclined to be friendly, cooperative, unselfish and trusting. People who are unrewarding are inclined to be more critical and guarded, willing to speak their minds and tend to be disagreeable and establish a reputation for being pessimistic, argumentative and confrontational. This reputation may help to demand high standards, but it will be a matter of time before it destroys relationships and the support that comes with them. It's important that these people provide an appropriate level of relational contact before giving someone something to do for them or asking others for help. Sharing knowledge and resources proactively and often without expecting anything in return will go a long way.

Control your temper

Enthusiasm and passion can very easily cross over to manifest into moodiness and excitability when the pressure is on. No one likes an immature complainer and in the world of business and those who become discouraged or disappointed when unexpected issues pop up are seen as undeserving of sitting at the adult's table. If you're one of those people who project too much emotion, think about the situations that trigger your feelings of frustration or anger and log your tendency to overact when a setback may come about. For example, if you turn on your computer at the office and there are 50 emails to read regarding a major project your team has been working on don't answer them immediately. Give yourself space and a little time to wait and calm down.

Another example is if someone makes a comment during a meeting that you find irritating, keep calm and control your reaction. Your transformation won't happen overnight, but you can side-step situations that are stressful and impede your reactions by sensing your triggers. Focus on working on becoming aware of your emotions not only in terms of how they are experienced but even more importantly how others experience them.

Don't take offense when receiving negative feedback

We all know and have to admit that criticism is difficult to hear and take. If you feel that you've worked extremely hard on a project or building a business and someone comes in and critically critiques what you've accomplished, it smarts.

However, criticism is quite often entrenched in truth, even when it's not delivered in a manner that you feel is ideal. When you are the recipient of negative feedback, you can either put your feelings aside and try learning from what you've heard or read, or you can exhibit anger and let your emotion get the better of you.

When we receive criticism regardless of whether it's delivered well or not, it's important to think of the following:

- Instead of concentrating my attention on the delivery, how can this feedback help me or my team improve and do a better job?
- Putting my own feelings aside, what is it that I can learn from this alternate viewpoint?

There are instances that you should tune out criticism, such as criticism based on falsehoods or delivered in a manner that is meant to tear down your sense of self-worth. In reality, however, that's not the usual case.

If the goal you are looking at is to do better, don't allow your mind to shut down to negative feedback because of your emotion. Rather, learn from the feedback.

Maintain a schedule

In order to be successful in self-managing yourself, you need to maintain a schedule and stick to it. It is extremely important if you want to finish your tasks efficiently. Scheduling appointment in your calendar is telling yourself you're going to do your tasks and complete them by an X date and it's going to take Y hours to accomplish. (RocheMartin, 2019)

Get Moving

Motion will get your body out of its routine. Get out for a walk, get to an exercise or yoga class or keep your mind busy with a book or a puzzle. Break you're the routine rut.

Eat well

Try to maintain a balanced diet because what you eat, and drink has a tremendous effect on your emotional state. Missing meals or eating unhealthy foods can put your body out of sync, and that can affect your mood.

Be interested

One of the key factors in being self-aware and managing your emotions and managing yourself is taking the time to show interest in the subject matter, regardless of whether it's business or personal. This is a good way to check on how you're reacting to what the subject matter is. It can be a business report that you must read but are struggling with it because it's boring and you'd much rather read the newest edition of your favorite magazine. (RocheMartin, 2019)

Trust

People will not trust you if you don't exhibit your trust in them. Developing trust with someone can be difficult to do and if it's lost, regaining it is hard. Remember that no one is perfect and we're all only human and mistakes will be made. Offering trust to a person is inviting them to offer their trust to you.

Have a healthy curiosity

People who have high emotional intelligence have a curiosity about things and about strangers. They are highly empathetic and take the time to learn more by talking with strangers about themselves and understand their views, opinions, and lives that are culturally different from our own. Next time you're in a setting that gives you that opportunity, seize it.

Networking

Speaking of an opportune way to get to speak to strangers and step outside of your comfort zone - a good way to do this is attending networking events. One of the great things about networking events is that there is a common reason for attending. Yet everyone comes from different walks of life. The common reason is the ice-breaker. After the introductions, it's time to stretch that curiosity muscle.

It's not what you say but....

The importance of non-verbal communication and how that impacts on someone's opinion of you. The way you stand, your body language, eye contact and your tone of voice are important in letting others know how you're feeling, what your mood is emotional. Once you've mastered the practice of getting your emotions intact, consider how you're coming across to others physically.

Do you cross your arms when someone is offering you or when you're offering feedback? It's a sign of resistance and protection. It is an attempt to put a barrier up between a person or something they don't like, conveying a negative, defensive, uninviting message. The opposite is an open stance with your arms relaxed at your side. It's the little gestures that convey your emotion even if you don't realize it. (RocheMartin, 2019)

Show humility

Sometimes you may feel you're surrounded by people who may not be as smart or are smart but not that quick to grasp an assignment while you've mastered it ages ago. This situation can have you exhibiting being self-assured that comes across as forceful, arrogant and someone who doesn't admit to their mistakes. Although there is an amount of self-belief when you're trying to climb your professional ladder can be seen as inspiring. However, the most effective leaders are those who don't believe their own hype and exhibit being humble about their abilities and knowledge. There is a healthy balance between modesty and assertiveness. The ability to accept feedback as well as to admit to one's errors is probably a task that can be difficult to grasp. When things begin to head south, people look to a confident leader but at the same time supportive and are taught with humility as they work to solve the problem and right the situation.

Developing this element of emotional intelligence, it's sometimes necessary to feign confidence and it's even more important to fake humility. The world we live in gives rewards to people who hide their insecurities, but it's imperative to hide one's arrogance. For some people, this is incredibly hard, and others don't even realize they come across in that manner. Hiding arrogance means looking for opportunities to recognize others even if you feel you're right and they're wrong, picking and choosing your battles and swallowing your pride if you're in the wrong and accept the responsibility graciously and correct the error.

What's the unknown?

When you're building your social skills the best way to do so is to get out and be sociable. This may sound simple, but it's not possible to strengthen your social skills without your being social yourself! Join a group that enjoys similar interests, like a book club or a museum touring group or network outside the usual circle of friends. It's the best way to practice and put all the tips you've learned about emotional intelligence into action. (RocheMartin, 2019)

A final note on how to boost your emotional intelligence:

Practice and practice again

Like all the things we learn in our lives, practice makes implementing all the pointers that you've read about in this chapter. Working and learning to improve your emotional intelligence isn't something that happens overnight.

If you consistently practice and use these tips as well as other pointers as a guideline will allow you to begin controlling the power of emotions and use it to work for you.

Chapter 9: Benefits of Emotional Intelligence

There are many benefits in learning and building your emotional intelligence. In the past, you may have made decisions in your life that did not quite end up the way you expected. You ask yourself questions like "Why did I do that? What was I thinking?" Not having or using your emotional intelligence can possibly be the reason your actions and decisions turned out to be not that good.

This chapter will review what we've already learned about emotional intelligence, and the benefits it provides in both your professional life as well as your personal life. There is so much that is impacted by learning and implementing the skills of emotional intelligence and there is even a section on how emotional intelligence is something to establish for your children as they can grow to adulthood so they can have healthy relationships and a productive life.

We know that emotional intelligence is our ability to acknowledge, comprehend and manage our emotions positively and effectively. People who nurture their emotional intelligence and manage their emotions well communicate better, have the ability to resolve conflicts, have diminished stress and anxiety, improve relationships, can understand others and empathize with them and overcome the challenges of their lives effectively.

Our quality of life is affected by our emotional intelligence because it impacts on our relationships and our behavior. Self-awareness is synonymous with emotional intelligence because it gives us the ability to conduct our lives with reason, intention, and autonomy.

Many of us navigate life by making decisions that are critical and based on what our current situation is. We may think of them as not being able to have things change. This limits our choices and solutions. When we take time to examine and understand why we the decisions that we do helps us to lead our lives decided by our conscious intentions instead of being driven by circumstances.

Self-awareness – is the basis of emotional intelligence. It is developing an internal barometer that lines up with and is harmonious with the world that is around us. It is the capacity to understand our emotions, moods, and drives that affect us, as well as their effect on those around us. (Dickson, 2019)

We are able to recognize, understand and label our emotions. When you have self-awareness, it necessitates us to "tune in" to our feelings and eliminate any negative emotions such as sadness, fear, and anxiety. The key to nurturing our self-awareness is to recognize our own emotional states and the way they impact our decisions, behaviors, and thoughts. (Durlofsky, 2018)

An example of someone who is not aware of their emotional intelligence gets angry at insignificant provocations in the workplace. This person is a team leader, whose angry eruptions impacts negatively on the morale of the team and diminishes their motivation.

Regulating our Emotions – Self-regulating is committing to being personally accountable for our emotions. It's better to regard our accountability as not a line you must hold yourself to, but as something to welcome. (Dickson, 2019)

When we regulate our emotions and have them under control rather than acting on impulse or in a destructive manner, we are able to avoid negative, unpleasant feelings in ourselves and imposing these feelings on others. In regulating our feelings, we are able to afford ourselves space and time to make decisions on how to diminish or alleviate the negative feelings and instead cultivate positive feelings and building our self-confidence. We are also able to have the ability to think through various solutions to a specific issue or problem. When we don't react only from an unregulated, knee jerk emotional standpoint, the results are much better in the outcome of our making any decisions. (Durlofsky, 2018)

Internal Motivation - people who are leaders that have a durable emotional intelligence can acknowledge their internal motivations and how they connect with the motivations of their team and organization. When you have a strong inherent motivation that is an advantage competitively in practically any business situation, and the capability to use that motivation to be successful cannot be undervalued.

The knowledge that helps highly motivated leaders make constructive decisions in their relationships and interactions with others is their knowing the prerequisites to fulfil those motivations and the crucial roles others take part in those achievements.

Empathy – The key component of any successful human relationship and the foundation of emotional intelligence is empathy, having the ability to understand the emotions and feelings of others. When we don't exhibit empathy, it is hard to how our actions impact on others. (Dickson, 2019)

Empathizing with others, we are basically "putting ourselves in their shoes." Their feelings are ones that we recognize as those we ourselves have felt in our lives and can commiserate with them.

When we empathize, we develop an intimate, deeper relationship with others. We are able to acknowledge why and how other people feel. Our behavior and actions influence other people as well as our own. Empathy augments our relationships, experience and a greater understanding of ourselves as well as the other people and world that surrounds us. (Durlofsky, 2018)

Social skills – social skills that are forward-thinking are invaluable assets to have as a leader. These skills are necessary to put all the insights, knowledge and empathy that you've nurtured into practice. (Dickson, 2019)

This phrase is a term that is very broad. Generally, when you have good social skills, it means communicating in a polite, concise and clear manner. It is the summary of all the emotional intelligence factors – emotional regulation, self-awareness, and empathy. These skills help you navigate situations that are challenging and establish mutually beneficial relationships. They help resolve conflicts and enhance communication.

Emotional Intelligence in the Workplace

When people are hired to a position in an organization, they are evaluated by their hard skills, their existing knowledge and education combined with an assessment of their personality.

The problem is that assessments to measure someone's personality is measured by four temperaments. Currently, the thought is to consider the right temperament for the right position is the possibility of being successful. As an example, an organization wants to hire extroverts for their sales force. They can hire an extrovert, but the assessment cannot measure the emotional intelligence of the possible candidate, so there is not a way to determine which one is persistent which is a good quality in someone making sales, and which one is insistent them means they won't take no for an answer and wasting time trying to make a sale to someone who won't buy. (Polman, 2010)

If an organization can evaluate the emotional intelligence of a potential candidate for a position and have the ability to look at the candidate's ability to handle stress, identify biases and control their emotions, they can be better matched with an organization's position.

Some examples of the benefit of establishing emotional intelligence in the workplace are:

More Sales – a Fortune 500 study of over 40 companies disclosed that salespeople that have high emotional intelligence achieved 50% more sales than those with medium and low levels of emotional intelligence

Better Productivity – The same Fortune 500 study discovered that tech programmers who were assessed in the top 10% of the emotional intelligence capabilities, were turning out new software at a rate of at least three times quicker than those techs with lower measurements.

Staff Stability – a Fortune 500 company had been using an assessment to measure personality traits for many years to reduce the high turnover of their sales force. This assessment was not doing the job. However, by integrating assessments that included emotional intelligence subjects like self-awareness, social skills and stress management and the company was able to halt the drain and turnover by 67%. This was a savings of approximately $30 million by their costs being reduced for recruiting and training and sales increases through retaining their sales force. (Polman, 2010)

Organizational Communication Improved - as studies of Canadian and U.S. companies discovered that firms who communicate with their employees outpace those who do not financially. A company with an excellent communications program provided a 475 greater return to shareholders than a company that had the least communicative program. (Polman, 2010)

Benefits of Emotional Intelligence Skill-Building for Kids

Skill-building programs aid individuals to develop their own personal awareness. Personal emotions as well as replying to the emotions of peers are included.

Children can be helped by developing emotional intelligence today as well as later in life by providing them with skills they need to succeed in managing their feelings, function well and solve problems that will translate into a successful adulthood.

There are five ways that building emotional intelligence in children will benefit them later in life: (Big EQ, 2017)

Interpersonal Relationships – When a child has strong emotional intelligence they are assisted in developing sound, interpersonal relationships by building empathy. Children who are able to empathize and see difficulties from another viewpoint become adults who are kind, congenial and flexible. People react well to empathy and tighter relationships are built throughout a child's life. Their relationships whether platonic, with family or romantic ones, will benefit from early emotional intelligence development.

Greater Problem-Solving Skills – A child can successfully analyze situations when they learn emotional intelligence. Having these skills will prepare your child with the tools needed to efficiently interact with other people. The better a person can comprehend people and analyze situations, the more effectively.

Life Satisfaction

All of us have experiences of life that can be upsetting, but when a child is taught emotional intelligence, it can help for them to be able to manage their emotions and better deal with their problems. They are able to make sound decisions and set goals that are achievable. When the child becomes an adult and has sound management of all aspects of their life, they are inclined to have a sound handle on every aspect of their life overall. All these skills set your child in a position to have higher life satisfaction as an adult. (Big EQ, 2017)

Greater Ability to Deal with Stress

Your child's future mental health can be helped by diminishing stress levels when the child builds emotional intelligence skills. Studies have shown that people in an environment that has a high-stress level; high emotional intelligence acts as a barrier. This barrier aids in strengthening the brain to enable the person to handle psychological stressors.

If your child grows up to engage in a career of medicine, for example, or another type of stressful field and has built their emotional intelligence over the course of their life, they are most likely to be strong and capable of handling the daily stress of the job.

Greater Job Performance

There is a 90% connection between those who have high emotional intelligence and high performance. By helping your child establish higher emotional intelligence, you are aiding them in the ability to increase their job performance in the future. Emotional intelligence has an impact on the future career of your child, job potential, job growth and salary by helping them to comprehend and work well with future coworkers and management supervisors. (Big EQ, 2017)

Many benefits can be derived from building your emotional intelligence. Your interpersonal relationships with romantic, familial and friends benefit, your ability to perform in the workplace as a productive person affects your management, coworkers and the world around you. You are able to interact with customers and clients, communicate clearly and concisely, and have the ability to grow in your professional life. When you regulate your emotions, you make sound decisions, have reduced stress and anxiety.

Children can benefit from learning emotional intelligence early in their lives. The skills of managing their emotions, better able to analyze situations, reduce their stress, i.e., taking tests in school or speaking in front of their classmates. A child can develop emotional intelligence and carry the lessons learned well into their adulthood and benefit in both their personal and professional lives.

Overall, you can benefit greatly when you have emotional intelligence incorporated in your life.

Chapter 10: Personal Productivity or Emotional Intelligence – Emotional Intelligence and Its Effects on Productivity

What effects does emotional intelligence have on our personal productivity and the productivity of others, or a business or organization?

We know that emotional intelligence is how we are able to read, feel and react to the emotions within ourselves as well as others. It is vital in being able to have a meaningful, personal relationship and it can have an effect on our productivity as well.

Personal Productivity

There are all sorts of books on productivity, seminars, blogs, lectures. Personal productivity, professional productivity. The list goes on.

The problem is that productivity doesn't work well if you're constantly stressed, analyzing and being analyzed every step of the way — not a really good place or to be and not a great feeling.

What is needed is a controlled emotional state, clear, concise decisions and not blind, hurried rationale.

To have smoother productivity and success, you need to understand your emotions and control them; emotional intelligence is what is needed.

The model for emotional intelligence is comprised of four elements

- o **Self-awareness** – you recognize your own emotions
- o **Self-management** – you control your own emotions

- o **Social awareness** – you are empathetic and understand the emotional processes that are happening in society and the world around you
- o **Relationship management** – you develop relationships, inspire people to change, and are able to manage conflicts

How Personal Productivity is Affected by Emotional Intelligence

- o Understand the role of emotional intelligence in your productivity and success. Take a test to see how emotionally intelligent you are.
- o Read more about emotional intelligence, or choose an article, seminar, video on the topic. There is more information about productivity in this chapter that can be applied personally as well as you being part of a team in the workplace.
- o Become socially responsible. Contribute to others, donate to charity, volunteer at your local ASPCA or nursing home. Do these things because it comes from the heart and not because you're supposed to or it looks good.

Pay attention to your workspace. You may be freelancing, but you still need to be organized in your workspace and surroundings.

Being organized helps you to be more creative in your thinking, improve and boost your productivity and have the ability to be in control, self-aware and successful.

Team Productivity

What is the difference between a team and a group of people working together? What about a team and a dream team? Businesses and experts consider one approach that takes from good ones to great. Emotional intelligence, a skill that has been an increasingly important part of individual and the development of group professionals.

Although emotional intelligence has been incorporated into the workplace since the 1990s, there has been a lag in the development of focus groups. Since then, professional emotional intelligence is now probably as vital as IQ (technical skill) for success in the workplace. In other words, the saying "It's not personal, it's business" can no longer apply. Studies have shown that real innovation and engagement arise from an investment in a task is a personal one. (Trello, 2016)

An Emotionally Intelligent Team

A healthy interpersonal emotionally intelligent team has three key conditions that are needed for the group to be effective: trust among all members in the group, a group identity and a sense of the group's effectiveness.

Your team can probably do the job they're assigned and get by without these conditions. However, can the pinnacle of your potential and understanding your work as efficiently as possible? Probably not. The reason there's an absence of having a dream team standing is not due to inexperience or a lack of technical skill but because the team members aren't relaxed enough to completely and fully engage with each other on an emotional basis and it affects the task at hand.

A group hug isn't quite the answer to this situation, but more of a lack of engagement between the team members and is a subconscious reflex that you all haven't been great friends since you were born. The other reason is that quite a few of the team members don't develop or work on these three key conditions of productive teams consistently.

This dream team idea has a lot of positive vibes going for it and you think it's a good idea. Concentrate on the following areas of group emotional intelligence and you'll begin to see the power of how emotional intelligence can be a positive:

(Trello, 2016)

Normalize Group Emotional Intelligence

The key to team emotional intelligence is with the Group Emotional Competence (GEC) Inventory. When there is a development of inventory norms into actual habits with the members of your team, there will be a set of patterns of behavior that the group will all accept that will promote trust, support, and understanding.

According to the GEC Inventory, there are nine specific norms that help to achieve emotional competence:

3 Levels	6 Dimensions	9 Norms
Individual	Group awareness of members	Interpersonal understanding
	Group management of members	Confronting members who break norms of behavior
		Caring behavior

Group	Self-awareness of Group	Team self-evaluation
	Self-management of Group	Creating resources for working with emotion
		Creating an affirmative environment
Cross-boundary (External)	Social awareness of Group	
		Organizational comprehension
	External relationships of Group management	Building external relationships

Source: http://www.eiconsortium.org/pdf/GEI_Technical_Manual.pdf

A team is developed from these norms from the first level, the individual level (each team member), as a group, and at a team-to-team level, like across all company departments. The focus on awareness and management of emotions at each level is are the dimensions of this development. (Trello, 2016)

Here are ways your team can become a normalized intuitive emotionally intelligent group:

Interpersonal Understanding

Group awareness needs to be facilitated at its most basic level by facilitating group awareness of each team member's personal comfort level with group projects and activities. When making group decisions it may seem the obvious thing to do by taking each individual's point of view into account, but just asking a general question like "What does everyone think?" isn't quite enough in a group setting.

Reviewing the members of the team, one team member may identify as an introvert and doesn't feel comfortable speaking in public, while another member of the team may begin a conversation and look at the negative side and then process the entire picture. Team member number three may be quick to start talking about all the big picture possibilities and proclaim it's an exciting project but isn't and isn't as sharp in focusing on the finer details of the project. As a team, everyone needs to acknowledge and accept that all of these points of view are important and valid toward accomplishing a successful goal

Perspective is the main factor. The responsibilities attached to the project needs that each team member does so, as well as be transparent about, taking each of their viewpoints into account.

Members who break norms need to be confronted

The team probably has a set of rules that indicate how team members need to treat each other. As an example, don't make people on the team feel bad or inadequate because they aren't aware of a fact or concept that others on the team might know already. If that happens unintentionally or not, the team member who breaks the norm of the group is confronted by other members of the team. In the example given, it was unintentional, but it wasn't okay based on the team's rules. An apology takes care of this type of situation then move on to the next fun topic.

It's not necessary to feel bad about breaking a group norm, especially if it's not intentional. Being heedful to call out and correct the mistake can be a way to make the team feel comfortable, is non-judgmental and emotional safety a priority.

Team self-evaluation

Assess the strengths and weaknesses as a team regularly. This can be accomplished with evaluation exercises or using a consultant as a third party or build internal feedback into the team meetings that are held weekly. Let the feedback be on a general basis involving the entire team. Look at things that are causing annoying setbacks, productive processes, and major wins and ways that you interact with one another.

Improving the team is the purpose of evaluation. Keep this goal, norms of interpersonal understanding, caring behavior, appropriate confrontation and understanding in mind when there are grievances to be aired or calling for processes to be changed.

Create an affirmative environment

It's great your team loves the work they do, but they also need to eat a serving of something sweet to help it go down effectively. An emphasis should be put on optimism as much as possible. As a team, be committed to always treat everyone's words actions and efforts as positive, good intentions for the group. This goes the distance in eliminating any worry or mistrust over perception.

Having an upbeat disposition doesn't mean you have to do stand-up. All it means is that your team operates from a place of being positive as much as possible.

Solve problems proactively

When you have an emotionally intelligent team, there shouldn't be any team member struggling with a problem by themselves. And a problem shouldn't be left unattended with an assumption that it's someone else's stress they'll have to take care of.

Problems being solved proactively as a team means that no man is an island, and no one does nothing when there's something that needs to be done.

Behave carefully

This is a simple, basic lesson that everyone probably needs to work on every now and again: Treat other people in the same way you prefer to be treated. Include compassion and empathy for personal struggles, recognizing each other's value and supporting the efforts of each of you putting into the shared goals.

Make sure you have each other's back! Please and thank you go miles in people feeling appreciated and respected. Take the time to have an interest in each other's state of mind and being. It doesn't mean you all have to be best friends, but you do have a vested interest in being great teammates (Trello, 2016)

Understand the organization

Your team may be together and in sync, but how does your team fit in the larger group? Teams that are close can turn into cliques and a group that is super-inwardly focused can make other groups within the organization feel as if they're at an arms distance and out of the loop.

Think about taking turns acting as the contact with other departments or field any external feedback on any major projects and initiatives the impacts the entire company.

Don't isolate yourselves as "that group" in the lunchroom. Keep your team open to other teams and individuals in the company and value their perspectives and experiences

Nurture external relationships

This is an excellent way to interact with other teams and individuals in the company. At monthly meetings, a different team can present their projects for everyone in the organization to get involved or offer ideas.

Empower others with your team's knowledge and expertise, while inviting others in the company benefits from your team's work.

Emotional intelligence should be an ongoing commitment to the productivity and well-being of your team. Before you know it, your whole team will be happy being involved and benefiting from the trust, support and understanding that was built that makes a group a dream team!

Chapter 11: Beliefs and Emotional Intelligence

Do a person's beliefs interact with emotional intelligence? People usually uphold their beliefs as unconditional truths, regardless of whether they can be proven or not. One person may believe that everyone is equal and should be treated as such while another person may believe that everyone should be fairly treated. Their beliefs form their views which they perceive and make sense of what those around them say and do. We all observe the situations and people around us based on what we believe. Beliefs are the foundation of many emotions functioning at once. (Greaves, Ph.D., Jean and Fullerton, M.S., Robert, 2019)

As an example, think about two people who are coworkers with apparently contrary beliefs. One person, Randy, takes his position seriously, works hard. He takes pride in his work and often-time puts in long hours because he is of the belief that his dedication to the job is reflected in the amount of time he spends working at the office. He is married and preparing to put his daughter through college next year.

The other person, Bill, is also diligent and hard-working but considers his work day to be a nine-to-five workday so he can be a coach a community softball team, dine with his family, spend quality time with his youngest child and enjoy family time. All his business accounts were well-managed, and his clients are happy with him. His production numbers are not at the top of the office, but he doesn't commit any more time to his position as he sees fit to accommodate his lifestyle.

Over time, Randy quietly became annoyed with Bill's casual approach toward work. All the other office personnel have united and worked together to achieve the goals the corporate office sets for their branch. Bill leaves at the dot of five every day. Randy thinks it's Bill's obligation to work longer hours to help their branch office achieve its goals. However, Bill is economical with his time, works the same hours as always and works at home in the evening after he spends time with his family and the kids are put to bed for the evening. His evening research gives him a head-start in the morning. Randy doesn't realize Bill is making an extra effort.

Both Randy and Bill's values are comparable. They both value their professional life as well as their family. However, each of them has a different viewpoint of what hard work is and which way is the best to take care of their family. Randy belief about what hard work is had him focus on the time that Bill ended his business day. Seeing Bill leave each day at 5pm makes Randy examine Bill's commitment to his job and arouses the emotions of resentment and bitterness because of his belief. Randy decides to avoid Bill in the office because his feelings lead him to believe their values aren't in sync. However, because of these resentful feelings, Randy unknowingly cut himself off to an alternate reason for Bill's comings and goings.

Our Behavior and Feelings are Driven by our Beliefs

When we get peeved because of someone's actions, our beliefs may be the reason why we respond that way rather than what the other person does that annoys us. If Randy had acknowledged that his feeling of bitterness was negative and counterproductive (his self-awareness) and that there was always a possibility that there was more to each person's story (social awareness), he may have spoken to Bill to find out what he was doing to help their branch office meet corporate's goals.

Many of our assumptions and what we anticipate come from beliefs like Randy's. Whether it's right or wrong, our beliefs blur our insight into situations that we are in and the people that are around us. The situation is not what decides how we feel but the way we see the situation based on what we believe.

Belief	Perception	Emotions	Behaviors
I put in the extra time to get the job done	You leave the job every day earlier than I leave	I feel resentful that you do your part to help achieve our goals	I resent you, so I'm going to avoid you and you make me feel bad

As we see a situation through the lens of what we believe, we have particular emotions that are aroused and, in turn, influences us in how we behave in a given situation

Recognize Unrealistic, Outdated, or Ineffective Beliefs by Using Emotional Intelligence

If there is a specific way we are viewing a situation and it arouses emotions that are problematic, it may help to go back and look at the basic belief we have in that situation. If you begin getting agitated over a situation with a person, it would be helpful to be self-examining first. When you recognize the emotional reaction, think of it as a signal from your body and mind that there's something off balance.

When you have this type of reaction, it could indicate that a belief that you hold has been violated. If it's an emotion that is causing you to be distressed and is strong, consider the way you perceived what's going on and how it may be linked to a belief. If you can, write down your belief as a statement.

Here are ways to uncover your belief, rethink it and adjust it, so the negative emotions are eliminated:

Uncover the belief –*sometimes work needs for everyone to go beyond their limits to accomplish the job and get it done*

By creating it as a statement and making it real, you will comprehend why you feel the way you do about the situation. It's possible to be able to give thought to alternative beliefs

Rethink the belief – *do I have to define hours at the office the only way of "getting the job done?"*

Sometimes, you'll make the decision to uphold your belief and take certain actions based on them. There will be other times you'll understand that your belief is creating a dispute in your relationship with your coworkers

Adjust the belief – *sometimes work needs for us to put in extra hours, but some people are able to accomplish more without having to put in any extra hours at the office*

Beliefs that are purposeless can be changed to adapt to changing practices at work

Handle Incompatible Beliefs with Emotional Intelligence

There will be times when a belief you uphold and is dear to you is not shared by others. The belief may be so essentially important to you that you neither want to adjust or rethink it is an option. As an example, you may have the belief that there are not bad people, just people attempting to do their best. However, your boss, who's a cynic, believes that people are just plain lazy and like to take short cuts. You have three choices to make in this case – you can address your boss' belief, live with his belief or leave.

The skills you learn from emotional intelligence will help you in making a constructive choice. You can make sure that people understand what you believe if you address beliefs that are incompatible with yours, so they understand your actions rather than indicating what's wrong with the other person's beliefs. When you live with it means accepting that it's okay not to agree on every issue and releasing the drive to change what the other person believes. You may emotionally disengage and focus on the job at hand. When there are beliefs that conflict and are essential to the work you do, the attitudes of your company or the relationship with your boss continued negative emotions may be your signal that it would be best to disconnect and remove yourself and find a position, boss or company that has compatible beliefs to yours. (Greaves, Ph.D., Jean and Fullerton, M.S., Robert, 2019)

Behavior is propelled by emotions and feelings, thoughts and beliefs. There is always a reason why we do what we do. Actions don't come about without cause and the causes are our emotions and feelings, our beliefs and thoughts.

For example, we may have a belief that someone should say "pardon me" if they bump into us. Our behavior may be activated from that belief. There are times that we are aware that our feelings and beliefs and there are other times when we are not conscious of what we're responding to. These may be unconscious, hidden beliefs or feelings.

There are causes for our feelings and beliefs – they come from the experiences that we've had. This goes right back to before we were born. There are incidents that happen to us and we develop ideas about ourselves as well as about the world as a result of those incidents. We generate feelings about our world and ourselves.

Our beliefs affect our emotions and in turn, affects our behavior. The beliefs that we uphold may or may not be of benefit to us and our emotions. An example is a member of your Wednesday evening book club meeting is habitually late, and not by a few minutes, but always by half an hour. You believe that if you've made a commitment to be a member of an organization and they meet every Wednesday at 7 pm, then you should be on time and not be very late every week. You feel it's discourteous and rude. She is a member that you only met through another member, and don't really know much about her. She is a nice enough person and a great contributor to the book discussions that everyone enjoys. You don't understand why this can't be corrected and are considering asking her to drop out of the group. The lateness is irritating, and you've been finding yourself having a difficult time speaking with her and are beginning to distance yourself from having and lengthy conversations with her when the club takes a snack break.

A few days later you run into one of your close friends who is also a book club member. You decide to stop and have a coffee and while you're talking about the next book the club will be reading, your friend mentions the tardy club member and says she won't be able to make the meetings any longer. This surprises and secretly relieves you. However, the reason she is no longer able to make the meeting is one you didn't expect to hear. You find out that she cares for her elderly mother and it's become too much for her to arrange for someone to stay with her while she attends the meeting. This is the reason why she's always so late. The only person she could get to stay with her mother can't make it until 7 pm, the same time the book club meeting starts. Now she's lost the person that was staying with her mother, so she has to drop out of the club.

Fortunately, you had not acted on your belief because of your emotion of being irritated at her being late. You learn that you need to pause, uncover the belief, rethink it and adjust it. A bit more of self-awareness and social-awareness is something you feel you'll have to work on. You may uphold your belief about others making a commitment and honoring a situation you feel is important to you, but you may want to rethink and adjust that belief and update it.

The correlation between our beliefs and emotional intelligence is one that takes time to understand and identify in our emotional reactions. We now know that we can either acknowledge a belief as one to uphold no matter what the situation or rethinking and adjusting a belief to consider the situation. The choice will be ours. We just have to recognize the outdated beliefs and those that are worth keeping. With practice and using our emotional intelligence, we can be successful in achieving this goal.

Chapter 12: Financial Crisis and Emotional Intelligence

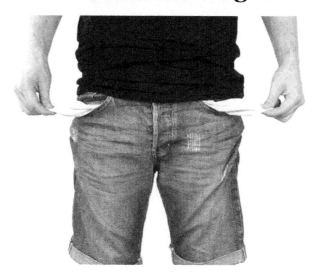

There are times in our lives that we are faced with a financial crisis, either on a personal level or via how the nation's economy is acting or reacting to national and world events that have an impact on the financial world as a whole.

There is a psychological process that motivates problems when a financial crisis arises and how the negative aspect of this type of situation can bring more fruitfulness and richness into our lives by using emotional intelligence.

Whenever there is a credit or financial crisis, the underlying psychology and ensuing recession is fear. Along with fear is greed, self-interest and, sometimes, a complete lack of integrity. This natural behavior is the outcome of feelings of inadequacy, resentment, fear, and guilt. These feelings come from a basic fear of shortage – the belief that there is not enough of what we need to have happiness is inadequate. It is the central matter that motivates competition.

Lack, or a shortage of anything, drives our needs and develops an entire assortment of negative behavior. Some people go into denial of what is lacking and emotionally become disassociated, distancing themselves. Rather than think through why there is a lack or shortage and how to turn a situation around and use their emotional intelligence of positive thought, there is a retreat instead.

In hard times, it is the instinct of humans to allow emotions and to be reactionary. This may have been helpful to us in the past, making us take flight from danger; it does not do well as effectively in a business situation. If you are a leader or manager, managing your emotions is an unbelievably valuable quality, especially during a time of crisis, especially one that touches on the financial segment of a company. (Illumine Company, 2013)

When you have the capability to have full, comprehensive thought processes that study all options through and thoroughly, and choosing the best strategy in a calm, confident manner makes all the difference in an outcome. This method would be in place of jumping at the first option and trying to make a possible square peg decision fit into a round hole issue, then try to force a resolution because there was no full thought process in deciding on this strategy. This would be a decision that is a rushed and panicked decision that can have overwhelming results during a crisis.

Having a high level of emotional intelligence can help you get away from situations that can be complicated and tricky, but they can also turn such a situation into opportunities. Recently, a study indicated that when the financial crisis of 2008 was at its peak, there was a downfall in the levels of emotional intelligence shown by managers. The researchers that conducted the study had thoughts that indicated the reason why there was such a downturn in emotional intelligence was that managers panicked and withdrew into their own emotional fear of lack and failure and focused on survival.

Instead of looking at what business opportunities were available and missing them entirely, the situation and the economy really got worse. If a manager was able to manage their fear throughout this time could have taken advantage of the scarcity of any competitors and build on opportunities. The study also showed that being too conservative while in a crisis can be as precarious to a company.

(Illumine Company, 2013)

There are some people who are, by nature, more emotionally intelligent than others. However, emotional intelligence can be learned and make a tremendous difference in how they can understand their emotional reactions in time of a financial crisis.

Emotional Intelligence Test

Reactions

The following two questions determine your emotional reactions.

Scoring: a – 3 pts. B – 4 pts. C – 2 pts. D – 1 pt.

1. When criticized, I:

a. Ignore the criticism

b. Listen and learn

c. Become defensive

d. Get angry

Scoring a – 1 pt. b. – 2 pts. c. – 4 pts. d. – 3 pts.

2. In a difficult situation I:

a. Get scared

b. Retreat if possible

c. Maintain a positive attitude

d. Let others take the lead

Total score for this section: _____

Responses

We react emotionally when we are faced with different situations

Scoring Questions 3 through 9 for each question:

a. – 1 pts. b. – 2 pts. c. – 3 pts. d. – 4 pts.

3. When working towards a goal, I am able to handle stress, anger, fear, and anxiety

a. Strongly disagree

b. Disagree

c. Neither agree nor disagree

d. Agree

4. I am able to use any criticism and feedback to grow professionally and personally

a. Strongly disagree

b. Disagree

c. Neither agree nor disagree

d. Agree

5. I can maintain a sense of humor at the appropriate times and places, not use sarcasm or hurt anyone's feelings

a. Strongly disagree

b. Disagree

c. Neither agree nor disagree

d. Agree

---

6. I have the ability to see things from someone else's perspective

a. Strongly disagree

b. Disagree

c. Neither agree nor disagree

d. Agree

7. I recognize how others are emotionally affected by my behavior

a. Strongly disagree

b. Disagree

c. Neither agree nor disagree

d. Agree

8. I am capable of expressing a complaint I have properly

a. Strongly disagree

b. Disagree

c. Neither agree nor disagree

d. Agree

9. I listen to others with understanding and patience

a. Strongly disagree

b. Disagree

c. Neither agree nor disagree

d. Agree

Total score _____

We can describe our emotional reaction when presented with a situation. The following questions help you to do so.

Scoring for Questions 10 through 12

1a. – 1 pt. b. – 2pts. c – 3 pts. d. – 4 pts.

10. I am self-motivated, and I have a good deal of discipline

a. Never

b. Sometimes

c. Often

d. Always

11. I am able to contain my emotions and I don't get irritated in stressful situations

a. Never

b. Sometimes

c. Often

d. Always

12. I make an effort to listen to other people's perspectives even if I believe I'm right

a. Never

b. Sometimes

c. Often

d. Always

Total score _____

Situations

Determine how you would react in some of the following situations:

Scoring for Question 13

a. – 4 pts. b. – 2 pts. c. – 1 pt. d. – 3 pts.

13. Two of your friends are having an argument. Your response is:

a. Try to help each friend understand the other's point of view

b. Avoid both friends until they stop fighting

c. Pick a side and bad-mouth the other person

d. Let both of them vent their emotions to you
Scoring for Question 14

a. – 4 pt. b. – 1 pts. c. – 2 d. – 3 pts.

14. Your friend tells you her mother died. Your response is:

a. Allow your friend to express their emotions and offer your
support

b. Convince your friend to go out somewhere with friends to get
their
mind off her loss

c. Give your friend some alone time

d. Spend time with her but avoid talking about their loss

Scoring for Question 15

a. – 4 pts. b. – 2 pts c. – 3 pts. d. – 1 pt.

15. You are faced with an unpleasant task. Your response is:

a. Make a plan and work on the task a bit every day

b. Put completion of task off until the last minute

c. Get the task over with as soon as possible

d. Not do the task at all

Scoring for Question 16

a. - 4 pts. b. – 3 pts. c. – 1 pt. d. – 2 pts.

16. You get involved in a heated discussion. Your response is:

a. Ask for a short break before resuming the discussion

b. Give in and apologize because you want to end the argument

c. Insult the other person

d. Get quiet and stop responding altogether

Scoring for Question 17

a. – 4 pts. b. – 3 pts. c. – 2 pts. d. – 1pt.

17. You get a bad grade even though you worked hard on an assignment. Your response is:

a. Think about ways you could have improved your work and gotten a better grade

b. Ask your teacher for a better grade

c. Criticize your own work and feel disappointed

d. Stop putting working hard on the assignments and decide the class is stupid and a waste of time

Scoring for Question 18:

a. – 4 pts. b. – 3 pts. c. 1 pt. d. – 2 pts.

18. A friend from work has an annoying habit and each day it gets more annoying and worse. Your response is:

a. Tell your friend about their annoying habit and why it bothers you

b. Make a complaint to their supervisor

c. Talk about your coworker's annoying habit

d. Suffer silently

Scoring for Question 19:

a. – 4 pts. b. – 3pts. c. – 2 pts. d. – 1 pt.

19. You feel overworked when your boss assigns you a big new project. You're already working on many other tasks and projects. You feel:

a. Worried that you will never get all the work done

b. Overwhelmed completely by the tasks before you

c. Angry at your boss because he is not noticing how overworked you already are

d. Deeply depressed and sure you'll never finish it all and meet the deadlines

Scoring for Question 20:

a. – 2 pts. b. – 3 pts. c. – 1 pt. d. – 4 pts.

20. The person with whom you are working publicly takes credit for a project that you worked hard on. Your response is:

a. Immediately and publicly confront the person about the ownership of the work

b. Take the person aside and tell them you want them to credit you when talking about your work

Score for this section_____

Add all points to see how high your emotional intelligence is

Emotional intelligence score is: _____

If your score is between 68 and 80:

You have an extremely high emotional intelligence. You have the skills to understand, interpret and act appropriately upon your emotions and the emotions of others. You deal effectively with emotional and social situations and conflicts, and you are able to express your feelings without hurting other people's feelings.

If your score between 60 and 68:

Although you have a relatively high score, there is room for improvement. Watch the reactions of others so you can determine when you are using your emotional intelligence effectively and when you're not. Look objectively at social and personal situations where emotions can run high. Analyzing your success will aid in improving your already high emotional intelligence even more.

If your score is between 48 and 60:

You fall in the mid-range when it comes to your emotional intelligence. Although you are appropriately responding in most situations, you still find yourself losing it sometimes. You also get impatient with others and sometimes feel uncomfortable in situations that are emotional. However, you shouldn't worry. You are still able to learn more about self-awareness and self-control to turn this around and help you reach a high level.

If your score is between 40 and 48:

Your emotional intelligence is somewhat low. You may struggle to manage your emotions when high-pressure situations present themselves or when you get angry. You have some work to do to improve your emotional intelligence level. Start by trying to express your emotions after you regain your composure and are calm. Read more about emotional intelligence self-awareness and self-control to learn some techniques that can help you with controlling your anger and emotions.

If your score is below 40:

Your emotional intelligence is extremely low. You are probably experiencing stress and anxiety daily. Additionally, you are probably having a hard time in school or at your workplace and not making the progress you desire.

Read about self-awareness and self-control and helpful tips that can help you begin to increase your awareness and bring calmer in your life and gain an understanding of how important it is to have emotional intelligence.

No matter how high or low your score, you can increase your emotional intelligence by learning more about how to respond in various situations. Emotional intelligence can help you perform better in your workplace or school.

Conclusion

Thanks for reading *Emotional Intelligence: The Essential Beginners Guide to Mastering Social Skills, Improve Relationships and Control Emotions (Social Skills, Anger Management, Enneagram, and Self-Discipline*. Hopefully, it was informative and provided you with all the information and tools you need to understand what emotional intelligence is and successfully begin to develop your own emotional intelligence.

This book was written to outline and guide those who are beginning to develop their emotional intelligence skills. In this book, we have outlined how important it is to have emotional intelligence, especially in this day of electronic communications and diminished interpersonal relationships. Although we can write an email, tweet or send a text, speaking with one another and developing the human one-on-one communication in person is what a good deal of what emotional intelligence is. We need to be aware of our self and our emotions and have self-control of them, develop our social awareness and relationship awareness skills.

Now that you've read this book, you can use it for as a guide to refer to as you develop your emotional intelligence skills. If you are just beginning, we encourage you to follow the tips outlined in the book and practice them. You will begin to see what a difference the practice will make in a short period of time.

Don't be discouraged if you don't see immediate results. As with learning anything new, it takes time and patience.

Finally, if you found this book useful in any way, a review on Amazon is always appreciated!

Printed in Great Britain
by Amazon

34593215R00089